COVENANT THEOLOGY

a reformed baptist primer

Douglas Van Dorn

COVENANT THEOLOGY

a reformed baptist primer

Douglas Van Dorn

Waters of Creation Publishing

1614 Westin Drive, Erie, Colorado 80516

Unless otherwise noted, references are from the *English Standard Version* (ESV) of the Bible.

Cover Design by Douglas Van Dorn

ISBN-13: 978-0986237607 (Waters of Creation Publishing)
ISBN-10: 0986237604

Also by Douglas Van Dorn through Amazon.com

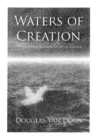

Waters of Creation: A Biblical Theology of Baptism
This ground-breaking study gives a Reformed Baptist argument for baptism from the continuity of Scripture via covenant theology. It shows the OT roots of baptism, along with a detailed analysis of how baptism fits into every OT covenant. Helpful charts included.

Galatians: A Supernatural Justification
This is a series of sermons preached on Galatians. They include a detailed exegesis of the book and a Reformed view of salvation. They also highlight the many supernatural elements of this amazing letter that are often overlooked in commentaries and sermons alike.

Giants: Sons of the Gods
An Amazon bestseller for the genre. *Giants* is a biblical theology on a topic that many wrongly believe is exhausted in the person of Goliath. This book is a worldview changer. It includes a semi-technical *Introduction* on the "son of God" from Gen 6:1-4 and several Appendices on extra-biblical literature and giants in the Americas.

Coming Soon...

From the Shadows to the Savior: Christ in the Old Testament
Originally a series of blogs for the Decablog, this book looks at the vital question of how Christ is in the Old Testament through things such as prophecy, typology, law, and numerous words that personify Him such as the Word, Glory, Wisdom, Son, and Name.

Gods, Ghosts, Giants, and Goblins
This book may be the first catechism on the paranormal or supernatural things in the Bible. It is written in a simple question and answer format, and as a story. It begins with God, deals with Satan, gods, idols, demons, giants, and eschatology. With Scripture proofs. A two volume commentary will eventually accompany it.

Contents

Preface

THIS BOOK BEGAN AS A SERIES of Sunday evening lessons on covenant theology between 2012-2013. As I put my notes on this daunting topic to paper, the result ended in this book. It is intended to be a primer on covenant theology rather than an exhaustive treatment. Some might say it is too detailed for an overview, but the scope includes the whole Bible, this is a complicated subject, and some things in it are too important to give a mere tip of the hat. I try to stay away from technical language. There are footnotes and a select Bibliography for those who want further investigation from a Reformed Baptist perspective.

My take on covenant theology is a little different than most. For example, I am a *Baptist*, so I believe that the only proper recipients of baptism are those who profess Christ. Most Baptists are not covenantal at all, and those who confess to be so are often ridiculed and mocked, because such a thing is often thought to be impossible. But I am *Reformed*, by which I mean to a large degree that my perspective is covenantal. Thus, my view of covenant theology informs my theology of baptism. However, as will be made clear, my view of credobaptism stems from my view of the *continuity* of Scripture via the covenants. I do not argue for believer's baptism from the differences between covenants, as many of my Reformed Baptist brothers do, though there are differences, as all covenant theologians admit, and these differences do have important implications.

Part of how I do this is by parsing covenant theology into six Old Testament (OT) covenants and one New Testament (NT) covenant. Most books on covenant theology see only five OT covenants. The sixth covenant is vital to my view of baptism, and also helps inform the relationship of the moral and ceremonial laws of the OT in a more consistent and straightforward manner.

The way I will go about our study is as follows. First, I will define covenant theology. Second, I will compare covenant theology with other systems of theology that Protestant Christians have used to organize their theological thoughts about God's word. Third, I will define "covenant." Fourth, I will talk about the importance of the unity of Scripture. Fifth, I will look at types of covenants in the ancient world. All of this is in preparation for a formal study of the covenants.

The biblical covenants will be grouped into four basic categories. The first is the *Covenant of Redemption*. This is the pre-temporal, intra-Trinitarian covenant made between the Father, Son, and Holy Spirit. This sets the groundwork for all historical covenants that follow, for all historical covenants flow out of this one. It is their fountainhead.

Next is the *Covenant of Works*, sometimes called the Covenant of Life or the Covenant of Creation. This is the first historical covenant. It is found in the Garden of Eden before the Fall of Adam and Eve.

This is followed by the six OT covenants which I have deliberately given the paradoxical title *Gracious Legal Covenants*. The point is not to confuse the law and the gospel, but to show that these OT covenants were rooted both in Israel's obedience to the covenant (following the idea of the covenant of works), and in God's gracious condescension to them via the unconditional promises of a future covenant (the Covenant of Grace), through the typological means of grace God provided for them in the meantime. As such, a person could approach each of these covenants via the line of law and works, or via the line of grace and gospel, which produces both faith and thankfulness that results in obedience.

What makes Reformed Baptist covenant theology different from its Paedobaptist counterpart is that we view the Covenant of Grace as being that covenant which comes through the person and work of Jesus Christ.[1] All gracious covenants in the OT had this covenant in mind *prospectively*, meaning, God looked into the future and, knowing that Christ was absolutely certain to accomplish the work he was given to do, gave grace to OT saints on Christ's behalf through means of grace that typified this coming work. These means of grace were always attached to covenants. But because of this, only when we come to the new covenant will we discuss the *Covenant of Grace* proper, the covenant Christ made with his church.

The final chapter contains several applications. Why does covenant theology matter? How does it relate to our worship, our understanding of the Bible, our view of salvation, our view of Israel, our view of the law, our practice of baptism and the Lord's Supper, and our view of children in

---

[1] See especially Micah and Samuel Renihan, "Reformed Baptist Covenant Theology and Biblical Theology," in Richard C. Barcellos, ed., *Recovering a Covenantal Heritage: Essays in Baptist Covenant Theology* (Palmdale, CA: RBAP, 2014), 475-506. An early version of this can be found at: http://thelogcollege.files.wordpress.com/2012/11/rb-cov-theo-renihans.pdf, last accessed 10-14-2014.

the covenant? These are both practical and important implications to which covenant theology directly speaks.

One of the things I like most about covenant theology is how, when done properly, it seeks to be as biblical as possible. Yes, it is a system (as we will discuss momentarily). Yes, we have to think theologically about it. But first and foremost, it is not about philosophizing or speculating or looking at traditions. It is about going to the Scripture to see how God speaks about Himself. Surely, one of the main ways he reveals himself is through the doctrine of covenants.

Very special thanks to Dave Neumayer for the diligent work on so much of this book. Thanks also to our former elder Sean Kielian, pastor Chris Marley, pastor Nick Kennicott, and others who looked over the manuscript before it went to print. Also, thanks to my amazing church that allows me to write for their benefit and for the benefit of others. Know that this book is already being used as a textbook across the seas to prepare men for Reformed ministry in places where Reformed Theology is almost unknown.

I pray that this study of covenant theology will be used of God to help clarify confusing matters and to lead you to a better knowledge of, and walk with, the Lord Jesus.

Doug Van Dorn ~
Reformed Baptist Church of Northern Colorado (Fall, 2014)

Covenant Theology Defined

COVENANT THEOLOGY IS A *system of biblical interpretation*. Everyone seeks to interpret the Bible. To "interpret" means to understand the meaning of something. Language interpreters seek to translate one language (say English) into another language (say Spanish) in a way that is faithful to the original without being wooden or stilted. This is both a science and an art. Bad translators do not know enough of the nuances of the two languages, and thus important things can become lost in translation. Covenant theology seeks to be a good translator rather than a bad one.

Covenant theology is a *system of biblical interpretation*. It seeks to be built not built on speculation or philosophy, but upon God's word. It does not merely interpret a verse here or a passage there, though of course it does this. Rather, it seeks to interpret the entire Bible. So covenant theology is like a map you pull out to figure out where you are going (or rather, where the Bible is going). Of course, this presupposes that the Bible is going somewhere. This is a reasonable assumption gleaned from the pages of the Bible itself. The Bible is a story, and all stories are going some direction. Covenant theology sees the idea of covenants as the unifying setting for that story.

The Bible can be overwhelming to understand. Interpreting the biblical data is for the purpose of understanding the whole. Therefore, covenant theology is a *system of biblical interpretation*. Systems combine many parts into a complex unit or whole. The parts of this system are the various covenants found throughout Scripture. God made covenants with Adam, Noah, Abraham, Levi, Moses, David, and Christ. These covenants relate in various ways to Israel and the church. Covenant theology seeks to discover the relationship of one covenant to another. How are they similar? How are they different? How do they work together, if at all? Thus, covenant theology is a system of biblical interpretation which organizes the Bible around covenants.

Systems of Theology

BECAUSE COVENANT THEOLOGY IS A SYSTEM, it is organized by men. But two things should be said about man-made systems. First, these systems can be helpful, so long as the system is itself rooted in the Scripture. The idea is never to have the system drive the Bible, but the Bible to drive the system. Scripture is the engine. The system is the body. We go along for the ride. Second, *everyone* has a system. It is naïve to think that anyone approaches the Scripture apart from some preconceived network of ideas. No one is an island of pristine neutrality when it comes to the Bible, not even the most hardened atheist or New Ager, not even the person who has never heard of the Bible, for even they have preconceptions about God and his world. The question is, where will we seek to derive our system from—Scripture or the imaginations of our own wicked hearts and fallen minds?[2]

Covenant theology is not the only Christian system for approaching the Bible. Other systems have arisen. These systems include but are not limited to dispensationalism, new covenant theology, kingdom theology, the heavenly/angelic divine council, and others. Some systems can be complementary to others. Some systems are incompatible with others. The debate between dispensationalism, new covenant theology, and covenant theology falls generally into the latter cat-

---

[2] This is not to say that using fallen tradition, reason, experience, or other things are not helpful and useful. It is to say that they must always be held in their proper place: under the authority of Scripture.

egory. To the degree that they speak about different things, or about the same thing in the same way, they could be complementary. But to the degree that these systems differ in their understanding of the same topic, they are contradictory. Ideally, each system seeks to derive itself from Scripture, but they can't all be right in the places where they differ on the same topic (though they could all be wrong).

Why have covenant theologians used the matrix of covenants? Why not something else, like dispensations? First, perhaps it is because in its most basic form, Scripture itself is written as a covenantal treaty. Covenant treaties were a genre of literature in the Ancient Near East. They followed a specific repeating recognizable pattern of *Preamble, Historical Prologue, Stipulations, Sanctions,* and *Successions.* The Bible also uses this genre. For example, the entire book of Deuteronomy is really an ancient covenant treaty.

1. Preamble (Deut 1:1-5)
2. Historical Prologue (Deut 1:6-4:43)
3. Ethical Stipulations (Deut 4:44-26:19)
4. Sanctions (Deut 27:1-28:68)
5. Succession Arrangements (Deut 29:1-34:12)

Many other parts of the Bible can also be read in such a way. Some are more explicit than others. The point is, the structure of the Bible is often covenantal.[3] Covenant is one of the Bible's own frameworks.

---

[3] See for example Meredith G. Kline, *The Structure of Biblical Authority* (Eugene, OR: Wipf & Stock, 1997).

The covenant treaty is the most basic form of literature in the Bible. It is basic not because it is the easiest to identify, or even the most widely used. It is basic because it comes first. Deuteronomy is the climax of what is known as the Pentateuch, the first five (*pente* means "five") books of the Bible sometimes called the Books of Moses. But not only does the Pentateuch end with a covenant treaty, it seems to begin with one as well. I will look here at Genesis 1-3. These chapters are a lot of things. In fact, taken together, they may be the most beautiful, complex, and multi-layered literature ever penned. Among the many things that they are, scholars have suggested that they may be read as a covenant treaty:[4]

1. Preamble (Gen 1:1-2)
2. Historical Prologue (Gen 1:3-2:3; 2:4-2:25)
3. Stipulations (Gen 2:16-17)
4. Sanctions (Gen 2:17b; 3:22), argument over sanctions (3:1-5), and judgment (3:8-19)
5. Succession arrangements (Gen 3:15; 21-24)

Moving outward, we discover that the book of Genesis contains the term "covenant" (*berith*) twenty-seven times, or about one tenth of all its occurrences in the OT. In the Pentateuch as a whole, we can discover the roots of every significant covenant made in the Bible. Some are prophesied. Most are made with historical figures. We will look in great detail at these covenants later on. For now, it is clear that the be-

---

[4] John M. Frame, *The Doctrine of the Knowledge of God*, A theology of lordship (Phillipsburg, NJ: P&R Publishing, 1987), 12-13; Michael Horton, *God of Promise* (Grand Rapids, MI: Baker Books, 2006), 90; Meredith Kline, *Kingdom Prologue* (Eugene, OR: Wipf & Stock, 2006), 13-14.

ginning of the Bible is deeply concerned with, and organized around, the idea of covenant. This is an important reason why covenant becomes a lens through which to read the Scripture. This is how the Scripture itself is organized.

Second, God's very existence is covenantal. How and why can this be? First, God is triune. He is not one being and one person, but one being existing in three eternally distinct persons. Thus, the persons must relate to one another. This relationship is one of selfless *commitment* to each person rooted in promises and oaths. "The LORD has <u>sworn</u> and will not change his mind, 'You are a priest forever after the order of Melchizedek'" (Ps 110:4).

Second, God's word is His oath (Heb 6:13-18). Making a covenant is sometimes called "swearing an oath" (Ps 89:3; cf. Luke 1:72-73). At some point in time, that which is sworn in the oath is "granted" (Luke 1:73). Thus, "covenant," "oath," and "grant" are related ideas.[5] The Father swore an oath to the Son, and this oath forms the basis upon which the Son performs his earthly works (Ps 2:7; 110:1, 4; John 5:36; Heb 1:5; 5:5-6; etc.). These promises and oaths take the form of obligations the persons voluntarily perform for one another out of their mutual love and honor for each other.

Promises and oaths are not the only way the persons relate, but they do form a foundation *upon* which they relate. They root the relationship in trust and love, much like a marriage ceremony with its promises and oaths form the basis upon which the rest of the relationship will work properly and harmoniously. In fact, marriage is not strictly speaking a

---

[5] On "oaths" as "covenants" in the ancient world see G. M. Tucker, "Covenant forms and contract forms," *VT* 15 (1965) 488–90.

mere contract, but a covenant--inaugurated in words and ceremony, and consummated (ideally) in blood on the wedding night. So, God's very existence is covenantal, and covenant helps us make sense of God's tri-unity.

Finally, God's relationship with mankind cannot and must not be understood properly apart from covenant. Because we are image bearers, we are by nature covenantal beings. If God exists covenantally, then the image bearers likewise relate to God covenantally. Covenant is how God establishes a relationship with mankind, be it an individual person or a group through a representative. God is the Great King and the image bearers are his vice-regents on earth. This is the origin of the idea in which kings relating to vassals through covenant treaties in the Ancient Near East originates. Ancient pagans did not invent the concept. Rather, the concept is embedded into the very fabric of our being and relationship to God.

Covenant forms the basis of our relationship to God as well as the grounds upon which that relationship functions. Without God's swearing an oath, there would be no guarantee of blessing for obedience, no certainty of threat for disobedience, and no hope for eternal life to those who trust in Christ by faith. God's words would be capricious and untrustworthy. But unlike the promises of the gods in pagan religions who often broke their covenants (Ps 82), God's covenants are grounded in his character and his nature: God cannot lie (Num 23:19; 1 Sam 15:29; Rom 3:4; Heb 6:17-18). God will not break his promises, but constantly remembers his covenantal oaths even when we break ours. Thus, covenant becomes a self-imposed structure that keeps God from destroying us.

For these reasons and more, covenant is how covenant theologians view the very fabric of Scripture. Covenant is a major structure upon which biblical revelation is built. It is not that we think covenant is the central *focus* of Scripture. Christ is the central focus of Scripture. But covenant is *the structure and language* upon which the revelation of Jesus Christ comes to us and out of which we can make sense of him. For Christ is not an abstract idea, but a person. This person relates personally to other persons. He does so through his oath, his covenant, his blood.

Defining "Covenant"

WHAT EXACTLY IS A COVENANT? Do you remember in high school or college when you were dating and your friends asked you if you've had "the talk?" The conversation went something like this, "So, where is this going? Anywhere? What are 'we' exactly? Do you love me?" A friend of mind calls this the D.T.R.—Define The Relationship.[6] Until his friends had had the D.T.R., he told them not to bother him with the trivial matters of dating.

You will find a plethora of definitions of covenant in the literature, but at its essence, this is what a covenant is. *A covenant is a formal definition of relationship between two parties.* Fred Malone gives this basic idea a little more formality, "A covenantal Baptist definition of a covenant [is] … a solemn promise or oath of God to man, each covenant's content being determined by revelation concerning that covenant."[7]

This formal definition comes when the one party approaches another party and swears an oath. The party approaching is usually a greater party (such as a high suzerain king to a lower vassal prince).[8] This is one of the things that

---

[6] Thanks to Rev. Keith Thompson for this word picture and definition which follows.
[7] Fred Malone, *The Baptism of Disciples Alone: A Covenantal Argument for Credobaptism Versus Paedobaptism* (Cape Coral, Fl.: Founders Press, 2003), p. 62.
[8] In the case of God, it is the Father who swears to the Son. It is not that the Father is "greater" than the Son, for they are equal in essence and being. Yet, the Son is begotten of the Father. Thus, the Father swears to the Son. See chapter: Covenant of Redemption (below).

makes a covenant differ from a mere contract. In contracts, parties are often equals.

When the second party swears covenant fealty and mutual commitments are made, a bond is created between them. This bond is almost always "cut" in blood in the Bible. For example, Jesus says, "This is the new covenant <u>in my blood</u>" (Luke 22:20). Blood is the life of the covenant (Gen 9:4; Lev 17:14). This gets at the root purpose of sacrifices. Like "blood-brothers" who cut their hands with a knife and smack them together, the blood of the covenant creates a spiritual, invisible but very real bond. There are other elements that are often present in covenants, and we will take a look at them throughout our book.

It is the creation of this bond which makes breaking the covenant so reprehensible and difficult to bear (again, much like a marriage when the vows are broken and divorce occurs). When God is involved in a covenant (as is the case in all the covenants we will survey in this booklet), this relationship is a dispensing of his kindness, goodness, and wisdom.[9] In other words, God did not have to enter into any covenants with us, but he did so because he wished to display his love and nature to his creation.

---

[9] Thanks to Dr. Richard Barcellos for this insight. It is similar to that of Nehemiah Coxe, one of the prominent Reformed Baptists of the 17th century. He writes that a covenant is "a declaration of [God's] sovereign pleasure concerning the benefits he will bestow on [man], the communion they will have with him, and the way and means by which this will be enjoyed by them." Nehemiah Coxe, "A Discourse of the Covenants," in *Covenant Theology from Adam to Christ* (Palmdale, CA: Reformed Baptist Academic Press, 2005), 36.

Unity of Scripture

ONE OF THE HALLMARKS OF covenant theology is its emphasis on continuity or sameness. Other systems such as dispensationalism and new covenant theology trade more on difference and discontinuity. It is not that the former *only* sees continuity or that the later *only* see discontinuity, but that these are the watersheds that move the systems. A watershed is something like the Continental Divide that famously runs through my home state's alpine landscape. You can literally be standing on the top of the 14,275 ft. Torrey's Peak in Colorado and have one foot standing in a place where all the water that lands there ends up in the Atlantic Ocean and the other foot on a place where all the water that lands there ends up in the Pacific Ocean. At the place you are standing, the water is not far apart, but at the end it ends up in opposite parts of the world.

Practically speaking, discontinuity as the foundational principle within a system has been responsible for everything from the belief that moral law in the OT does not apply unless it is repeated in the NT (new covenant theologians often say this with regard to Sabbath questions for instance), to the belief that the two Testaments actually speak about two completely different gods (where the OT god is usually this angry grey-haired fuddy-duddy and the NT god is a nice, loving, hippie Jewish carpenter). Certainly not everyone stressing difference rather than sameness goes this far, but it cannot be denied that it is a person's watershed that leads to such conclusions. Those who emphasize the sameness of the Testaments do not reach such conclusions.

While there are differences between covenants and not all covenants are of the same kind, they are all still covenants. This adds complexity to the system, but not to the point of making it impossible to understand. God always deals with mankind the same way—on the basis of covenant. This is an important point if we hope to reach a unified, cohesive, biblical theology. The Bible is not a bunch of disparate unrelated parts; the New Testament is not God's "Plan B" (as if God made a big mistake); the same God speaks the same basic things in both Testaments.

Types of Covenants

IF THERE ARE DIFFERENT KINDS of covenants, what are they? There are two basic kinds of covenants found in the Ancient Near East. Scholars have referred to these covenants as *royal grants* and *suzerainty treaties*. The latter occurs when, after a great victory, the great king (the suzerain) approaches the lesser king (the vassal) with a covenant treaty. Here, the lesser king pledges entire loyalty whereby if he fails to keep the stipulations imposed by the agreement, he will fall under its sanctions or curses. If he keeps his word and fulfills his obligations, he will receive great blessings which are also guaranteed in the treaty. As someone has said, this is a "do or die" type of covenant.[10]

Royal grants are a bit different. They still generally occur after a great victory, but this time the parties are treated more like family (father/son or king/prince) than political allies (suzerain/vassal or lord/servant), though both ideas can be present simultaneously. In a royal grant, the heir is the beneficiary of an inheritance that arises from the beneficence of the great king, who wants to be kind in order to glorify himself. It is not unlike the movie *300* when Xerxes woos the hunchback Ephialtes into giving up the position of his Greek kin. If the victory is secured by this information, the king will give "every happiness you can imagine, every pleasure

---

[10] Michael Horton, *The Christian Faith: A Systematic Theology for Pilgrims on the Way* (Grand Rapids, MI: Zondervan, 2011), 537.

your fellow Greeks and your false gods have denied you I will grant you. For I am kind."[11] There was no formal curse here for Ephialtes, just a grant. Grants are part of what makes the great king "great." Thus we see that "In the royal grant, the emphasis is upon the suzerain's pledge or promise of reward. In the suzerain-vassal treaty, the emphasis is upon the vassal's obligation of loyalty."[12]

Moving this into the realm of redemptive history, we find that these same general covenantal pacts exist in the Bible. The equivalent of the suzerainty treaty is a covenant dependent upon obedience to specific commands with rewards and curses that follow from obedience or disobedience. They are conditional for the vassal in that if he wants to gain the blessing, he must perform some duty. If he doesn't, then he will face severe consequences. The maintaining of the blessing is perpetually conditioned in the future by continued obedience. Royal grants are unilateral gifts, not beholden to any future obedience but merely the good pleasure of the benefactor. Here, the obligation rests upon the suzerain to carry out his promise as a Father would to a Son. To generalize even more using the traditional language of covenant theology, suzerainty treaties are covenants of works, while royal grants are gracious covenants.

It shouldn't surprise us however that it doesn't always work this neatly, this black and white. That is part of the difficulty in trying to figure out exactly what to make of any given historical covenant. It is one of the big reasons why

---

[11] Nunnari, G. (Producer), Snyder, Z. (Director). (2007). *300* [Motion picture]. United States: Legendary Pictures.

[12] Bob Gonzales, "The Covenantal Context of the Fall: Did God Make a Primeval Covenant with Adam?", *Reformed Baptist Theological Review* 4.2 (July 2007): 11 n.30.

even covenant theologians disagree amongst themselves sometimes. Is covenant *x* a works covenant, a suzerain treaty; or is it a gracious covenant, a royal grant; or might it have elements of both, and is that even a possibility? To make sense of this complexity, covenant theology has spoken of *three* basic covenants in the Bible, rather than the two we have just looked at. They have been assigned theological names.

We have just spoken of the two most familiar categories: Covenant of Works and the Covenant of Grace. Both of these are *historical* in nature. That is, they take place between God and mankind in time and history. The third category is a *pre-historic* covenant. That is, this covenant was made "prior" to creation, in the fountain of the Godhead. Thus, the parties in this agreement are not God and men, but the persons of the Godhead. This covenant has been called the Covenant of Redemption.

Here is where it gets a little confusing, but if you can understand the basic idea, it will go a long way to helping you work through the different covenants of the Bible. The prehistoric Covenant of Redemption contains the seeds out of which *all* historic treaties and grants (works and grace) would be planted. It is the archetype for all kinds of covenants.

To put it another way, the Covenant of Redemption is actually worked out in history in successive stages (see diagram).

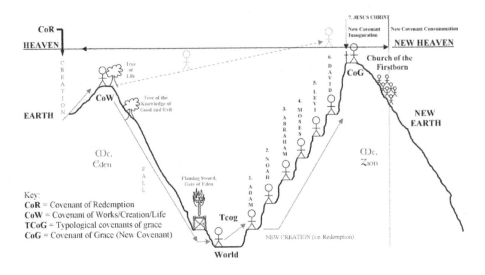

The first stage is the initial giving of the Covenant of Works. Here, the works of the lesser party form the legal basis upon which blessings or curses of that covenant ensue. This covenant continues in one form or another until the end of the age.

The second stage is a typological stage wherein all OT covenants are founded upon a single gracious future promise of Christ, yet they also maintain a works oriented aspect (as just defined) because the Covenant of Works was broken and has yet to be fulfilled. This works aspect can have two parts. The first and proper part is temporal, temporary, and corporate. If Israel wants to stay in the land, they will obey God. The second part is eternal, permanent, and individual. If someone wants to gain eternal life through works, that is fine, but they have to meet the covenant conditions perfectly. This is based on justice and fairness.

The third stage is the inaugural stage of the Covenant of Grace as it comes to us through Christ. Here the Covenant of Works is now obeyed, and thus fulfilled perfectly (Christ enters into the works arrangement seen in the second stage) so that God may offer the promises free of charge without any compromising justice to any that will bow the knee to Christ in repentance and faith. "Bowing the knee" or having faith is the "condition" of this covenant. No one enters into it apart from this. Faith here is in Christ's work on my behalf. Faith in his works forms the legal basis upon which blessings ensue. While faith is a condition, it is not the same as saying it is a meritorious work. In fact, it is just the opposite. At this stage, works do not cease to be part of the covenant (God always expects and demands obedience, even in heaven). But rather than my own works which form the legal basis upon which God would grant eternal life, it becomes the works of someone else on my behalf.

The final stage is the consummated stage of the Covenant of Redemption, complete with the fulfillment of the Covenant of Works and the Covenant of Grace. This is the heavenly-eternal stage when all of the blessings will be realized in their fullest sense. What I want to do now is look at these covenants and their stages in greater detail.

Covenant of Redemption

Biblical Basis

LET'S BEGIN WITH THE BIBLICAL basis for the Covenant of Redemption. Throughout the Gospel of John, Jesus says things like, "If God were your Father, you would love me, for I came from God and I am here. I came not of my own accord, but he sent me" (John 8:42). "The works that the Father has given me to accomplish, the very works that I am doing, bear witness about me that the Father has sent me" (John 5:36). "I have come down from heaven, not to do my own will but the will of him who sent me. And this is the will of him who sent me, that I shall lose none of all that he has given me, but raise them up at the last day" (John 6:38-39). One theologian summarizes it this way saying that Jesus had been given "a commandment to obey (John 10:18), a righteousness to fulfill (Mat 3:15), a baptism to be suffered (Luke 12:50), and a work to finish (John 17:4)."[13] With these works Jesus performs, the Father is well pleased (Matt 3:17; John 8:29), for his works are perfect (John 8:29; Heb 4:15). These verses seem to move us far ahead in our discussion to stage three and the Covenant of Grace, but two important features are relevant here.

First, Jesus said that he was "sent" to do this work. This sending took place in heaven sometime prior to his coming to earth. His coming was voluntary; he was not forced to do it.

---

[13] Kline, *Kingdom Prologue*, 139.

Yet, it was prompted by the sending of the heavenly Father. To be sent voluntarily means that they had entered into an agreement with one another. Completing the triune nature of the work, the Holy Spirit comes upon Christ at his baptism (Matt 3:16; Mark 1:10; Luke 3:22; John 1:33), much like he came upon the temple in the OT (Ex 40:34-35; 1 Chr 7:1-3; cf. Isa 63:10-11),[14] in order to empower Christ to begin his priestly work (work that we will say more about later). The Holy Spirit is also sent by Jesus and the Father after the resurrection to the disciples to continue Christ's work (John 15:26; 20:22; Acts 2:38). The Holy Spirit was not forced to come, but came of his own desire and volition. All of his work was part of a triune agreement. Therefore, the parties of this agreement are the Father, the Son, and the Holy Spirit.

Second, this agreement guaranteed some specific things. Jesus Christ would be a king and have a kingdom. This is found in the Psalms and other places. David, speaking of Christ (Acts 2:35) says about this Father and Son pact, "The LORD (*Yahweh*) says to my Lord (*Adonai*): 'Sit at my right hand, until I make your enemies your footstool'" (Ps 110:1). There are two Lord's here; both are greater than David. To put this another way, it was a covenant grant from the Father to his Son. This grant would be given to the son if he won the victory over that (and those) whom he came to conquer, namely—sin (1 John 3:8), death (1 Cor 15:26), and the devil (John 16:11; Rom 16:20; 1 Cor 15:24).

---

[14] For Jesus as the NT temple see John 1:14 where he "tabernacles" among us and John 2:21 where his body is the "temple."

In Psalm 2, this same promise is made, but this time it is said to be "decreed." "As for me, I have set my King on Zion, my holy hill. I will tell of <u>the decree</u>: The LORD said to me, 'You are my Son; today I have begotten you. Ask of me, and I will make the nations your heritage, and the ends of the earth your possession'" (Ps 2:6-8; cf. 82:8; 89:34-37). As Earl Blackburn says, this is "the decree the Father made with the Son to resurrect and enthrone the Son to status as the Redeemer and Mediator."[15] Again, this decree takes place long before Jesus is born of a virgin. The NT tells us that this was "the eternal purpose" of God that he has realized in Christ Jesus our Lord (Eph 3:11). In other words, it began in eternity past.

Besides being a king, the agreement was also that Jesus would be a high priest over a royal priesthood. "The LORD has sworn and will not change his mind, 'You are a priest forever after the order of Melchizedek'" (Ps 110:4; cf. Heb 5:6). We have seen how "swearing" is related to covenant, and this oath is likewise made long before Jesus comes as a man to earth.

Finally, Jesus would also be the Prophet to the world, the one who would speak God's truth to the ends of the earth. "I will raise up for them a prophet like you from among their brothers. And I will put my words in his mouth, and he shall speak to them all that I command him" (Deut 18:18; cf. Acts 3:22; 7:37). These three offices will have profound effects later on in the discussion.

---

[15] Earl M. Blackburn, "Covenant Theology Simplified," in *Covenant Theology: A Baptist Distinctive*, ed. Earl M. Blackburn (Birmingham, AL: Solid Ground Christian Books, 2013), 27.

There are several places we can see this whole arrangement as a covenant within the Godhead. Jesus literally says as much at the Last Supper (the covenant meal) when, after giving the "new covenant in my blood" to the disciples adds, "Just as my Father has <u>granted</u> me a kingdom, I <u>grant</u> you" (Luke 22:29). "Grant" is explicit language of the royal grant covenant idea. In fact, the word Jesus uses is *diatithemi*, the verb to which the noun *diatheke* (Greek for "covenant") relates.[16] It could just as easily be translated, "Just as my Father *covenanted* me a kingdom..." Given what we have just seen, this covenant was made prior to his coming to earth.

This idea of granting a kingdom through a previous covenant is present early on in Luke's Gospel. Zechariah, the father of John the Baptist, prays for God "to show the mercy promised to our fathers and to remember his holy covenant, the oath that he swore to our father Abraham, to grant us" (Luke 1:72-74). His prayer will be fulfilled in Jesus. When God spoke the covenant promises to Abraham, it says he spoke them to Abraham and to his seed (Gen 12:7). At one point, the Apostle Paul takes this "seed" to be Jesus (Gal 3:16). This means that God covenanted with Jesus at least as far back as the days of Abraham. Paul is saying that God spoke *to Jesus*. He also seems to have done it in the days of David, as the Psalms references in the previous paragraphs tell us. A classic text for all of this has been Zechariah 6:13 where the LORD speaks to the Branch (i.e. Messiah) "a council of peace," peace that extends beyond the Persons of

---

[16] Kline, *Kingdom*, 139.

the Godhead to others whom they will covenant with in history.

Reformed theology does not see the beginning of this covenant between the Persons of the Trinity as originating in the days of David or even Abraham. It sees it as pre-temporal, that is, before time began. This seems necessitated by other passages. For example, in 1 Peter 1:19-20 Christ is, "The lamb without blemish or spot ... foreknown <u>before</u> the foundation of the world." To refer to Christ as a lamb is to refer to him as a sacrifice and this is inseparable from the idea of covenant, since the sacrifice is the thing that seals the oath in blood. This means that the oath for Christ to accomplish his work on the cross had to be made before time began. That oath is sealed in time by Christ's own blood.

But this gets much more personal than the bloody idea of sacrifice. The foreknowledge spoken of here is not just God looking down the corridors of time to see what will (or might) happen. It is knowledge based upon a sovereign plan and love. "Foreknowledge" and "lamb" language speak intimately about Christ's profound love for his bride. Foreknowledge means, as Dr. James Boice says, "That God 'sets his special love upon' a person or 'elects' a person to salvation.."[17] He gives the example of Amos 3:2, "You only have I known [Hebrew, *yada*] of all the families of the earth." This is not talking about bare knowledge, as if God didn't know any other families existed. It refers to setting a special love upon this family. This "knowing" is where the NT idea of foreknowledge comes from. Then there is the idea of the

---

[17] James Montgomery Boice, *Romans: The Reign of Grace*, vol. 2 (Grand Rapids, MI: Baker Book House, 1991–), 921.

church, which is the bride of the Lamb (Rev 19:7-9; 21:9). Thus, we have in this covenant the roots of marital intimacy, how Christ knew us and loved us intimately even before the world began. As Arthur Pink says, "What assurance would be ours if, when we approached the throne of grace, we realized that the Father's heart had been set upon us from the beginning of all things!"[18]

A similar passage to the 1 Peter text is found in Revelation 13:8. The NIV has "the lamb slain <u>before</u> the foundation of the world." Most translations have the "before the foundation of the world" refer not to the lamb, but to those whose names are written in the book of life. Thus the ESV says, "Everyone whose name has not been written before the foundation of the world in the book of life of the Lamb who was slain." Referring to a book of life with names written before the world began is found throughout Scripture (Ps 69:28; Dan 12:1; Eph 1:4; Rev 17:8; etc). Either is grammatically possible.

If the former is the case, it parallels the idea in 1 Peter that we have just seen. If the later is the case, it bolsters the element of certain people who were chosen to receive the saving benefits of grace before time. This is explicit in Ephesians and other places. For example, "He chose us in him before the foundation of the world, that we should be holy and blameless before him. In love he predestined us for adoption as sons through Jesus Christ, according to the purpose of his will" (Eph 1:4-5). When we combine these ideas of a lamb slain prior to creation, names written in a book of life prior to

---

[18] Arthur Walkington Pink, *Exposition of the Gospel of John* (Swengel, PA: Bible Truth Depot, 1923–1945), 925.

creation, and the work of Jesus to obey his Father in all things and to lose none of those given to him by the Father, we end up with the central idea of our covenant and the reason why it is most often called the Covenant of Redemption.

Understanding Redemption and Its Application

Since theologians have given it this title of a Covenant of *Redemption*, and since redemption has vast complexity to it, we need to spend some time talking about what this covenant was purposed to accomplish. Redemption comes through Christ's work on the cross in time, prefigured in the OT by types and shadows. The following might get a little technical, but bear with it. I believe it is important to try to grasp.

First, there are several Greek words that translate earlier Hebrew ideas. The first is *lutroō*. The second is *lutron*. Notice the similarity. *Lutroō* is usually rendered as "redeem" in English (LXX: Ex 13:13; 34:20; Lev 19:20. NT: Luke 24:21; Tit 2:14; 1 Pet 1:18). Hence, "redemption" (and the reason why we are talking about it under this idea of a Covenant of Redemption).[19] *Lutron* translates the Hebrew *kōphar* and is usually rendered as "ransom" (LXX: Num 3:46; Ps 69:18. NT: Matt 20:28; Mark 10:45).

"Ransom" and "redeem" are not identical, though they do overlap. When we talk about a *ransom*, we usually refer to the thing being offered ("the ransom was a million dollars") or the one offering the ransom ("he paid the ransom"). In this case, the ransom is Christ's sacrifice and the one offering it is

---

[19] *Lutroo* translates the Hebrew *padah*, which we won't talk about here. Sometimes *padah* is also rendered as "ransom" (see next sentence).

Christ on behalf of his Father. However, when we speak about *redemption*, we usually refer to the one being redeemed (the person acquitted or let go). To put it another way, the former word speaks objectively while the later speaks subjectively. Both aspects are vital in this covenant, though they are very often merged together. More on this in a moment.

We need to add two more Hebrew words, because they have the same Hebrew spelling as *kōphar* (same consonants, different vowels). The first is *kaphar*. This is usually translated as "atonement" in the OT (Lev 6:30; 8:15; 16:20), but also "cover" (Gen 6:14) and "reconcile" (Lev 6:30 KJV; 8:15 KJV; 16:20 KJV). The only time "atonement" occurs in the NT (KJV), it gives the Greek *katallagé*," where it means "reconciliation" (Rom 5:11).[20] The other Hebrew word is *kippur* (from which we get Yom Kippur or Day of Atonement).[21] The Greek equivalent is *hilasmos* or the English "propitiation" (Rom 3:25; 1 John 2:2; 4:10). Sometimes it translates as "mercy seat" on the Ark of the Covenant.[22] Note the similarities again in *kōphar*, *kaphar*, and *kippur*.

Summarizing (see also chart below), in this one English word "redemption" we cover a wide range of ground: *redemption, ransom, atonement, covering, reconciliation,* and *propitiation.* Christ's work touches on all of these ideas. A thorough study of these words is beyond the scope of this book, but it

---

[20] The word also appears in Rom 11:15; 2 Cor 5:18-19 but is never rendered "atonement."

[21] *Kophar* and *kipper* are closely related in Ex 30:12-16 and in 2 Sam 21:1-14. The second text makes it clear that *kipper* can mean "to pay a *kopher*." (See Leon Morris, *Apostolic Preaching of the Cross*, p. 162-63).

[22] "Mercy seat" is *hilasterion. See Heb 9:5.*

is important to see the scope and complexity in order to make sense of the Covenant of Redemption.

Complexity of "Redemption"			
Greek Term		Hebrew Term	English Translation(s)
Same Family } *lutroō*			redeem
lutron		} *kōphar*	ransom
	Same Family }	*kaphar*	atonement, cover, reconcile
hilasmos		*kippur*	propitiation, mercy seat
katallagé			reconciliation

Now that we have seen that there is complexity, we can begin to make sense of these things by simplifying a bit. Here, we will look at a basic sketch of the two aspects of redemption hinted at a moment ago with "ransom" and "redeem." These are what I will call the subjective and objective aspects of the Covenant of Redemption.[23] They are not identical, but they do overlap. These two purposes have a narrow and a broad range of people in mind respectively. Since many people speak as if the Covenant of Redemption *only* has the narrow group in mind (i.e. the elect for eternal salvation), we need to discuss both aspects.

The first part is the subjective one, or what some have called the application to an individual. By application we

---

[23] These are categories given by Shedd who speaks of "Atonement as Objective" and "Atonement as Subjective." See William Greenough Thayer Shedd, *Dogmatic Theology*, ed. Alan W. Gomes, 3rd ed. (Phillipsburg, NJ: P & R Pub., 2003), 699-711.

mean something like this: "God redeemed me. I'm saved." Most people think of redemption in terms of this personal salvation. This is redemption's *subjective* aspect, because the one who receives salvation is the *subject*. As the Apostle puts it to the Corinthians, they are "reconciled to God" (2 Cor 5:20). This application of redemption/salvation was guaranteed to the elect in the Covenant of Redemption, for as we have seen, the Father gave unto the Son a people whom he would save from their sins. Therefore the words relating to redemption (above) have profound and personal application to these people once they are sovereignly and graciously brought to faith and justified in Jesus Christ. Faith is that which brings redemption to any particular subject (person).

This subjective element can be thought of in another way—namely as the reward provisionally *granted* by the Father in eternity to the <u>Son</u>, and subsequently *earned* by his <u>Servant</u> in history (as I intentionally mix the family [son] and political/work [servant] metaphors together, because Jesus is both). The reward includes a kingdom, kingship, and for our purposes here, a peculiar chosen people whom he will rule over, officiate over, and speak truth to for all eternity as a Brother, a Groom, a Lord, and as Prophet, as Priest, and as King. All of this is done so that the Son might be glorified for his works, even as he glorifies his Father who sent him to do them (John 17:4-5).

Thus, God will save the elect because he has chosen before the foundation of the world to do so in the Covenant of Redemption. Jesus death on the cross procured this "especially" for them (1 Tim 4:10). He did so because it both pleased him, and because he knew that none would accept his offer of reconciliation given their prior hatred of him in their sinful, depraved, unregenerate condition. People can't find God for the same reason that a robber can't find the police.

This means that there is something *effectual* in the death of Christ and in the Covenant of Redemption. That effectual thing is Jesus' intention to save all those given to him by the Father. Thus it says, "Christ gave himself for the church" (Eph 5:25), and he "lays down his life for the sheep" (John 10:11, 15). Subjectively then, redemption extends to a host of people ("as the stars of the heaven") chosen before the foundation of the world according to the decree of God in election.

The second aspect is one often neglected today (though not always in the past), when the atonement and this covenant are discussed.[24] People sometimes think of what we will say here as being contradictory to subjective redemption, but

[24] Cf. Paul Hobson [signatory First London Baptist Confession 1644, 46], *Fourteen Queries and Ten Absurdities About the Extent of Christ's Death, the Power of the Creatures, the Justice of God in Condemning Some, and Saving Others, Presented by a Free-willer to the Church of Christ at Newcastle, and Answered by Paul Hobson a Member of Said Church* (London: Printed by Henry Hills for William Hutchison Book-seller in Durham, 1655), 101-102; Charles Hodge, "Beman on the Atonement," *Essays and Reviews*, (New York, Robert Carter & Brothers, 1857), 175, 181-82; *Systematic Theology*, 2:544-62; Robert Lewis Dabney, *Five Points of Calvinism* (Birmingham, AL: Solid Ground Christian Books, 2007), 60; *Syllabus and Notes of the Course of Systematic and Polemic Theology* [sometimes called *Lectures*], Second Edition (St. Louis: Presbyterian Publishing Company, 1878), 527-28; Shedd, *Dogmatic Theology*, 742-43; see also Zacharias Ursinus, *The Commentary of Dr. Zacharias Ursinus on the Heidelberg Catechism*, trans., by G. W. Willard (Phillipsburg: P&R, 1994), see especially comments on Q. 37 (and see also how the language of the Orthodox Catechism Q. 36 is not changed even knowing Ursinus' comments on it); and John Davenant [a prominent member of the Synod of Dort], "A Dissertation on the Death of Christ," and "The Controversy," In The Epistle of St. Paul to the Colossians vol. 2 (London: Hamilton, Adams, and Co., 1832), 308-568, http://archive.org/stream/expositionofepis02dave#page/310/mode/2up, last accessed 10-23-2014. These and others from Augustine, Athanasius, and Chrysostom, to Zwingli, Luther, and Calvin, to Westminster Divines like Twisse, Vines, and Scudder and other notables such as Ussher, Bunyan, and Edwards can be found at http://calvinandcalvinism.com/?page_id=7147, last accessed 10-23-2014.

there is no formal contradiction here, for it speaks of Christ's work in a different sense, and a formal contradiction would only exist if it spoke of contradictory things in the same sense. This is the *objective* aspect of redemption and its associated words. This objective aspect is the removal of all *legal obstacles* on the part of the offended party. God is the offended party. The removal of all legal obstacles does not automatically save anyone, as can be seen by the fact that even the elect are "objects of wrath" (Eph 2:1-3). To think this is to hopelessly confuse the objective with the subjective.

The objective aspect of this covenant contemplates the legal or just punishment for sin, what Christ underwent for sin, and then compares those two things. As the term ransom indicates, the focus is on the thing paid or the one paying it. It contemplates sin rather than particular sins (any and all particular sins are included under the category of "sin"). It contemplates death.

The legal punishment for sin is death (Gen 2:17; Rom 3:2). Does it matter who commits the sin? No. All sin, and therefore all sinners, deserve death. Christ's satisfaction has to be able to cover the punishment for sin, any sin, all sin, no matter who commits it. What did Christ do on the cross? He died. This is just the point of the objective aspect of this covenant, as there are not two different kinds of death that Christ would have to suffer, one for the one group of people and another for another group. His death satisfies God's *justice* for sin. Thus, John Bunyan could write,

> A surety must consent to the terms of the agreement,
> or covenant; and so did Christ Jesus. Now that which He
> did engage should be done for <u>sinners</u>, according to the

terms of the <u>covenant</u>; it was this—1. That there should be a complete satisfaction given to God for <u>the sins of the world</u>; for that was one great thing that was agreed upon when the covenant was made (Heb 10:5, 17). 2. That Jesus Christ should, as aforesaid, bring in an everlasting righteousness to clothe the saints (His body) withal (Dan 9:24, 25). Here is grace" [underline mine].[25]

It makes no sense from an objective, legal point of view to say that Christ's death was for some people but not others, because the focus is on sin rather than particular sins (of certain individuals). Thus, the Bible can say that Christ died "for the ungodly" (Rom 5:6) or "for us" (Rom 5:8). How many people are counted as ungodly? All people. In other words, Jesus didn't have to *do* something more for one person than he did for another. His death was objectively as good for one person as for another. This was all contemplated in the Covenant of Redemption prior to Christ coming in the flesh.

Thus, the objective work of Christ in this covenant has a broader range of people in mind that the subjective aspect. This is like the Day of Atonement in the OT. The sacrifice was, objectively, for the entire nation, even though not all were chosen by God to be saved; not all would trust in the shed blood to forgive them of their sins. But it was sufficient to cover the sins of anyone.

The scope of those in mind in the objective sense asks the question, "Who has offended God?" Mankind has. All have sinned (Rom 3:23), not just a select few. Mankind has offended against God by breaking his laws and treasonously

[25] John Bunyan, *Doctrine of the Law and Grace Unfolded*, vol. 1 (Bellingham, WA: Logos Bible Software, 2006), 526.

rebelling against his Sovereignty. Justice demands that they must be punished. How many men? *All* men. With what punishment? Death (Gen 2:17; Rom 6:23). What did Jesus do on the cross? He died.

Jesus' punishment is what all men, not just some, deserve. Jesus' death satisfies the demands of justice against sin. With this in mind, part (but as we have seen, certainly not all) of the pact in the Covenant of Redemption was to send the God-*man*, the second *Adam* to remove the legal barriers that stand in the way of any man (human/man/*adam*) being reconciled to this God with whom they have broken covenant. As we have seen, this was done especially for the elect, but it does not preclude any human objectively speaking by virtue of the fact that they are—*human, adam*. What election does is guarantee that many who would not otherwise be saved will be. Yet, in Christ, God was reconciling the world to himself (2 Cor 5:18). If any man would come, he could be forgiven, because justice has been satisfied. The problem is, they won't come unless compelled.[26]

---

[26] The reason why people will not come is an entirely different matter from what we are speaking about here. We generally speak about depravity when it comes to the reasons for not coming to Christ. Depravity is a moral quality, a moral disposition found in all humans. It prevents people from *wanting* to come to God. Depravity does not speak, however, to our natural faculties in and of themselves. That is, God gave us minds to understand the gospel and wills to choose what we want to do with his offer of salvation. Jesus' death does not give anyone a new physical brain. Because he has given us these natural biological faculties, we can say that everyone has the natural ability to come to Christ. Hence, everyone is responsible to do so. The problem is, apart from the sovereign work of God ... no one "wants" to. (Reformed people do not deny the existence of the will, just its ability to act neutrally outside of the totality of our nature). But now that Christ has taken away the legal problem between God and man, God is now legally able to bring anyone he pleases to faith in Christ. This is the effectual aspect of the death of Christ we spoke about under the subjective aspect of redemption. This is particular (special) redemption. On the distinction between the natural and moral ability see Thomas Manton, "Sermons Upon 1 Peter 1:23," in *The Complete Works of Thomas Manton* (London: James Nisbet &

If we confuse the subjective and objective here, one line of reasoning (either the subjective or the objective) or the other will seem incoherent. This is really the fight that Arminians and many Calvinists have been having for centuries. But if we maintain the distinctions, both make sense, though not in the same sense. The elect are not *saved* in eternity past ("eternal justification" is a grave error). Nor are they saved at the cross, for again if that were the case, they could not be under the wrath of God prior to faith in Christ (Eph 2:1-3). They are justified during their actual lives through faith alone in Jesus Christ when the Holy Spirit "in time does actually apply Christ to them" (*1689 London Baptist Confession* 11.4). This was made certain by the plan of God for them, but also in the removal of legal obstacles at the cross which pertains to all people.

This seems to be the idea behind Calvin's thought that, "The Son of God was not content merely to offer His flesh in full measure to appear before the judgment-seat of God his Father in the name and in the person of *all sinners* ... Our Lord would have to suffer for the *redemption of mankind* ... When, then, we see that God summons *all those who have deserved eternal damnation* and who are guilty of sin and that He is there to pronounce sentence such that they have deserved ... it was necessary that our Lord Jesus Christ by himself without aid sustained such a burden ... He has sustained and borne the condemnation which was pronounced by God His Father *up-*

Co., 1873), 21:332. The same distinction was made as long ago as Augustine in *A Treatise on the Spirit and the Letter* 53: "Volition and Ability" where volition (the will) is the natural faculty and ability is the moral faculty.

on us all."[27] Calvin is not thinking subjectively—as if God is going to save everyone, but objectively like Bunyan—the legal barriers have been removed.

Jesus as "man" and "Adam" would die in some sense for mankind. That's the point of such an identification. Christ will share in all people's humanity, not just some people. Again, all men deserve death and Jesus died; thus justice *as it regards the penalty* has been paid in full. What more did he need to do? Did he have to do something different for those that would not be brought to salvation? These questions introduce us to the broader idea of this covenant that is often not considered. Jesus' sacrifice is acceptable to God for anyone who would trust in it, because it is this sacrifice alone that propitiates God's wrath, and it is a sacrifice offered by one who shares our nature. It removed the legal necessity for anyone to have to offer up a sacrifice (be it an animal or their good works) on their own behalf. This was part of the pact he entered into in the Covenant of Redemption, for it is unthinkable that Jesus would so something in the flesh that had not been thought about prior to his coming.

Thus, objectively speaking, in the atoning death of Christ as planned in the Covenant of Redemption, God has shown himself favorable towards *mankind*, since the demands of justice against sin—any and all sin—have been satisfied in the death of Jesus Christ, the second Adam (i.e. *man*). A great example and illustration of this is original sin. Christ died for original sin. But there is only one original sin, not many. Adam committed original sin, not us, but all humans inherit the

---

[27] John Calvin, "Sermon 3: Matthew 26:36-39," in *Sermons on the Deity of Christ*, (Audubon, NJ: Old Paths Publications, 1997), Sermon 3, Matt 26:36-39, pp., 52, 55, 60, and 65.

guilt of Adam's sin. It is imputed to his descendants, one and all. Either Christ died for original sin or he did not. If he did, then Christ's death satisfies the law's demands regarding original sin. Not some original sin, since there is no such thing. Thus, original sin need not legally hinder a person from being saved as it respects the law's demands. Anyone with original sin could trust Christ and be forgiven.

Objectively, as it regards humanity apart from salvation, this favorable disposition is shown to all by God in his giving of common grace to all human beings—the rain falls on the just and the unjust (Matt 5:45). God has given all living humans a temporary reprieve of eternal doom in order to show his kindness, tolerance, and patience, which are there to lead them towards repentance (Rom 2:4). God does not delight in the death of the wicked (Ezek 18:23; 33:11). He has made a way whereby any who would want can be saved, and he offers it to all who hear, free and without charge. And so on.[28]

God is able to justly dispense such kindnesses because Jesus' death makes such benevolence and grace both just and *justifiable* (Rom 3:25-26). Thus, as the old Puritan Thomas Watson said, "Now God hangs forth the white flag and is willing to parley with sinners."[29] There is nothing more, objectively and legally speaking, that God needs to do to save

---

[28] One of the more helpful little works showing this dual aspect of Christ's death, and in particular the temporary benefits and blessings it procures for mankind, is R. L. Dabney's *The Five Points of Calvinism* (Harrisonburg, VA: Sprinkle Pub, 1992), 60-67. He says, "The realized results of Christ's sacrifice are not one, but many and various" (61). Dabney does not get into the Covenant of Redemption here per se, but does in *Syllabus and Notes of the Course of Systematic and Polemic Theology*, Second Edition (St. Louis: Presbyterian Publishing Company, 1878), 429ff.

[29] Thomas Watson, *The Doctrine of Repentance* (Carlisle, PA: Banner of Truth Trust, 1987), 87.

anyone. It is sufficient for all. Any *could* come to him if they so wished, and God would be perfectly just to save them. God calls all who hear the gospel to do this very thing. And God, in his overwhelming grace, actually regenerates his wrath-burdened enemies—his elect—so that they will in fact turn to Christ and be justified.

Summarizing redemption as both subjective and objective is Dr. William Shedd who said, "The atonement *and its application* are [two] parts of one covenant of redemption between the Father and Son" [emphasis mine].[30] Shedd's immediate predecessor, and one of the "three great Reformed theologians" of the mid 18th century according to Reformed historian John DeWitt, Henry B. Smith says the same thing, "As applied in the Covenant of Redemption, that between the Father and the Son, it sets forth clearly, for popular representation, that in the divine plan, Christ performs conditions and his people are given to Him in consequence. (Only in this Covenant there should be included all that Christ's work accomplished: Propitiation for the sins of the whole world and the General Offer of Salvation as well as the Provision for the Elect.)"[31]

We fail to do justice to the Covenant of Redemption when we fail to deal with both of these aspects. As the old pre-Reformation (Lombardian) formula, accepted by all of the Reformers says, "Christ's death is sufficient for all, but efficient for the elect." This was first made possible in the Covenant of Redemption.

---

[30] Shedd, *ibid.*, 746.
[31] Henry B. Smith, *System of Christian Theology*, 2nd ed. (New York: A.C. Armstrong and Son, 1884), 378.

Objections

A word needs to be said about objections to this Covenant of Redemption. Many people do not see this covenant at all. They think it is nothing but abstract speculation grounded in a wrongheaded desire to be guided by the secret decrees of God. Sometimes, I suppose, some people have made this a valid objection. I've met my share of self-taught, internet learned, "Reformed" gurus who are obsessed with decrees (the hidden will of God), but have little desire to show much love to people (the revealed will of God). But the biblical reality is exactly the opposite. Rather than bare decrees that could be seen as abstract, capricious, and aloof, it is covenant that makes them personal, concrete, and loving; for it roots the decrees in the personal relationships of the Godhead.

Others say this is all system driven, an attempt to impose some unbiblical grid over the biblical data. As we have seen, our defense of this covenant has only been biblical. We have appealed to nothing else, and we have only just scratched the surface. But we have gone far enough to see that there is in fact good biblical reason to view a covenant as existing between the persons of the Trinity.

What I will look at next is how this pretemporal covenant works its way into history. In fact, the Covenant of Redemption is prerequisite for the main categories of covenants found in history and the various administrations of those covenants in time. Without this covenant, the other covenants do not exist or make sense, either separately or in conjunction with one another. This covenant undergirds them; the fullness of each covenant flows out of the plans, performances, and purposes of the Godhead in the Covenant of Redemption.

Covenant of Works/Life/Creation

Historical Preparation

A BRILLIANTLY AND PERFECTLY CUT rare diamond is price-less and has many facets. The opening chapters of Genesis are the Hope Diamond of the Bible. They are so pure, so rich, so radiant in their color and refracted light, so perfectly cut that the whole Bible can be seen as a commentary on them. People have considered the genre here to be poetic, subversive-mythic, scientific, apologetic, biographic, historic, liturgic, theologic, templatic (a word I coin to show that it is the template of a temple), and other things. None of these would *necessarily* be wrong, so long as they all remain in harmony with one another and consistent with authorial intent. Another of these facets is to see Genesis 1-3 as a covenant treaty, specifically a suzerain-vassal treaty. We have given the outline of this idea already. Now let's explore it a little further.

In the Babylonian Creation Epic—the *Enuma Elish*, discovered in 1849 in the ancient ruins of the Library of Ashurbanipal at Nineveh—the god Marduk fights the goddess Tiamat, the deified ocean and personified chaos monster (similar to Leviathan[32] or Rahab[33]), and creates the world from her body. It is depicted as a war and a great victory after which Marduk is elevated to the head of the pantheon. It has many similarities to the biblical story of creation, so many in

---

[32] Isa 27:1.
[33] Job 26:12; Ps 89:9-10; Isa 51:9.

fact that people reading it for the first time are often taken aback. It is also a classic precursor to suzerain covenant treaties. Because of the many similarities, when read against this backdrop, creation is to be understood as Yahweh's great victory (though for him, there was nothing difficult about it like we see in Babylon). Six days of work are the LORD's victory over chaos and darkness. Day seven is his enthronement as king in his great temple.[34]

One of the often missed covenantal features in Genesis 1 is the activity of God. Throughout the story, God "calls" things and gives them names (cf. Gen 1:5, 8, 10). The act of calling is the sovereign act of a king. It is also a covenantal act. Throughout the rest of Scripture, "calling" by name and "covenanting" go hand in hand. "Behold, my <u>covenant</u> is with you, and you shall be the father of a multitude of nations. No longer shall your name be <u>called</u> Abram" (Gen 17:4-5). "God said, 'No, but Sarah your wife shall bear you a son, and you shall <u>call</u> his name Isaac. I will establish my <u>covenant</u> with him'" (Gen 17:19). "I am the LORD; I have <u>called</u> you in righteousness; I will take you by the hand and keep you; I will give you as a <u>covenant</u> for the people, a light for the nations" (Isa 42:6). In the story of creation, God calls us "man" (Gen 1:26-28), and in what many people believe are the covenant wedding vows, Adam calls his wife "woman" (Gen 2:23).

Covenants are also full of blessings (and curses if they are disobeyed). Indeed, blessings are necessary ingredients in covenants. For example, "And because you listen to these

---

[34] See John Walton, *The Lost World of Genesis One: Ancient Cosmology and the Origins Debate* (Downers Grove, IL: InterVarsity Press, 2009).

<u>rules</u> and keep and <u>do</u> them, the LORD your God will keep with you the <u>covenant</u> and the steadfast love that he swore to your fathers. He will love you, <u>bless</u> you, and multiply you. He will also <u>bless</u> the fruit of your womb and the fruit of your ground, your grain and your wine and your oil, the increase of your herds and the young of your flock, in the land that he swore to your fathers to give you" (Deut 7:12-13). Throughout the creation story, God is said to bless (Gen 1:22, 28; 2:3). In language that directly recalls Genesis 1:28, God blesses Noah in the context of a covenant (Gen 9:1; 9-17). So with these ideas in place, is it right to call the opening verses of Genesis a covenant? It is.

Biblical Basis as a Covenant of Creation/Nature

Let's try to understand what kind of covenant these chapters exemplify. Jeremiah refers to God's "covenant with the day and the night" (Jer 33:20, 25), language that harkens back to the Flood covenant (Gen 8:22), and creation before that (Gen 1:5; Ps 74:16). Thus, the Bible explicitly says that there is *some kind* of covenant here. In other biblical commentaries on creation, the authors sometimes view it as a great victory, especially over the monsters Leviathan and Rahab (who represent evil, chaos, and Satan in the Bible).[35] Genesis is therefore giving us the covenant that arises out of this victory. For this reason, the covenant prior to the Fall is sometimes called the *Covenant of Creation* or the *Covenant of Nature*.

---

[35] As noted above.

This covenant with creation is based on the oath of God which "binds"[36] the forces of nature by natural *laws*. Curiously, the word for an "oath" is the same word for "seven" in Hebrew—שׁבע, the very number that completely dominates the opening chapter of Genesis.[37] Natural laws are referred to as God's "decree" (Jer 5:22), "ordinances" and "rule" (Job 38:33) over the creation. Creation was to be regulated and ordered by these laws.

The concept of "law" is key here. A breach of this covenant meant releasing the forces of nature which could destroy creation (Gen 9:9-17).[38] Salvation through the chaos of nature was thus seen as God's covenant faithfulness (Gen 6:18-22; cf. Ps 18:16-17; 69:1; 93:4; etc.).

---

[36] The close association between "covenant" and "bind" is seen in the German language where "covenant" is *bund* and the verb "binding" is *binden*. The middle Assyrian noun *biritu* also means "bond" or "fetter."

[37] There are seven days; seven formulas ("and God said," "and it was so," "and God made," "God saw that it was good," "God called," "God blessed," "evening and morning") repeated seven times; the first verse contains seven words in Hebrew, the next has fourteen (2 x 7). God ("elohim" occurs 35 times or 5 x 7); and many, many more examples. See U. Cassuto, *A Commentary on the Book of Genesis Part I: From Adam to Noah: Genesis I-VI*, trans. Israel Abrahams (Jerusalem: Magnes Press, 1961 [1944]), 12-13; and my sermon "Temple Building," Genesis 1:3-2:3; http://www.rbcnc.com/Genesis%201.3-2.4%20Temple%20Building.pdf, last accessed 10-14-2014. Making this very point in the covenant made between Abraham and Abimelech (Gen 21:27-31), Martin Luther says, "Accordingly, in this passage the word שׁבע has both meanings: both swore and, if I may express myself in this manner, both 'sevened.'" Martin Luther, "32. So They Made A Covenant At Beersheba," in *Luther's Works, Vol. 4: Lectures on Genesis: Chapters 21-25*, ed. Jaroslav Jan Pelikan, Hilton C. Oswald, and Helmut T. Lehmann, vol. 4 (Saint Louis: Concordia Publishing House, 1999), 86.

[38] Cf. Gen 1:26 and the creation of the sea monster Leviathan along with God's subduing the sea monster Rahab in Ps 89:10 and the close association of God's covenant in vv. 3; 28; 34; 39; also Job 26:12-13. This all becomes imagery used for God's covenant faithfulness to Israel in the Exodus; cf. Isa 51:9-10, which becomes a new creation (Deut 32:10-11. In these verses, two words—"waste" [*tohu*] and the eagle-bird that "hovers" [*rachaph*] are found only here and in Genesis 1:2 in the writings of Moses, thus giving us a deliberate connection that this is to be viewed as a new creation).

With Jeremiah 33:20 and 25 and the supernatural Leviathan and Rahab in mind, the Bible seems to connect this covenant in some mysterious way to the angels (cf. Job 38:31-33,
esp. vv. 8-10). In the Bible and the ancient world outside of
it, angels were intimately linked to creation as beings that
have derivative control over it.[39] God made a covenant with
the angels, a covenant which some of them[40] transgressed
(Gen 3:1ff; Isa 14:12-14; Ezek 28:13-15; 2 Pet 2:4; Jude 6;
Rev 12:4). Jews prior to the NT certainly saw this covenant
with creation as also relating directly to the angels and used
language reminiscent of Job 38 to tease it out.[41] So the idea
that there is a covenant here is truly ancient. More generally,
angels are also closely related to covenants as those that help
put them into effect (Jdg 2:1; Mal 3:1; Acts 7:53; Gal 3:19).

Biblical Basis as a Covenant of Life

But the central focus of this covenant has to be God's
image bearer—Adam. Part of man's (and this includes wom-
en) responsibility in the Garden was to have dominion and
subdue the creation, not in the sense of destroying and
wreaking havoc, but in the sense of being God's steward and
overseer (Gen 1:26-28). This is the "work" he was to do (Gen
2:15, 19-20). This work can be related to the offices of
prophet, priest, and king. As God's prophet, Adam was to
speak and apply the word truthfully in all of life (Gen 2:19-

---

[39] For example, Revelation 16 and the bowls that are poured out by angels.

[40] Perhaps all of them, which is why it may talk about "elect angels" (do you need to be
elected if sin is not an issue?; cf. 1 Tim 5:21) and says that even the heavens are not pure
and God's holy ones and angels are charged with error (Job 4:18; 15:15; 25:5). But this is
speculative.

[41] For the explicit Jewish idea see 1 Enoch 5:2-4; 69:13-25; Prayer of Manasseh 1:1-4.

20, 23).[42] As God's priest, Adam was to serve and to guard (Gen 2:15) the holy mountain and garden he was given.[43] As God's king, he was given dominion and rule over the creation (Gen 1:26-28).[44]

As the image bearer, Adam can be called God's son. Yet, like a prince trying to prove himself worthy, the King awaits his son's testing by fire to see if he will make a worthy lord. Thus, in the overall structure of the covenant treaty, the stipulations and sanctions of the covenant read this way, "You may surely eat of every tree of the garden, but of the tree of the knowledge of good and evil you shall not eat, for in the day that you eat of it you shall surely die" (Gen 2:16-17). The command is negative, "you shall <u>not</u>." If he eats, then he dies. Death is the punishment. The idea of physical death (which occurred later; Gen 5:5) must never be separated from its typological role of imaging to our senses spiritual/eternal death. The former points to the later and demonstrates its reality.

The opposite is implied in the stipulation "You may surely eat," especially from the tree he is made aware of called "the Tree of Life" (Gen 2:9). The blessing of life is implicit in the name of the tree. After the Fall, God says that Adam must not be allowed to stay in the Garden lest he eat from the Tree of Life and live forever (i.e. have eternal life; Gen 3:22). Eternal life is made explicit in connection to this

---

[42] The opposite is Gen 3:1ff.

[43] Genesis 2:15 has two words usually translated "work" and "keep." These two words are used together (cf. Num 3:8) in the rest of the Pentateuch in the context of priests "serving" (Num 4:23, 24, 30, 35, 39, 43, 47) or angels "guarding" (Gen 3:24) the tabernacle or holy place (cf. Num 3:7-8; 8:25-26; 18:5-6; 1 Chr 23:32; Ezek 44:14).

[44] See Bob Gonzalez, "The Covenantal Context of the Fall: Did God Make a Primeval Covenant with Adam?", *Reformed Baptist Theological Review* 4.2 (July 2007): 4-32.

tree at the end of the Bible (Rev 22:2-5). Because life is held out as the reward, this covenant is sometimes called the *Covenant of Life*.

Biblical Basis as a Covenant of Works

Genesis is not the only place that refers to Adam as being in a Covenantal relationship prior to the Fall. Isaiah seems to have this in mind when he says, "The earth is also polluted by its inhabitants, for they transgressed laws, violated statutes, broke the everlasting covenant" (Isa 24:5). This covenant is transgressed by everyone on earth, not just Israel, so it can't refer to Abraham or Moses. Again, men transgress this covenant in the same way that nature and angels do. They break God's laws. In fact, angels will also be punished in the same chapter wherein we see the people transgressing the covenant: "On that day the LORD will punish the host of heaven, in heaven, and the kings of the earth, on the earth" (Isa 24:21). This may tie the two groups to a single covenant. Like the covenant with the day and the night, this covenant could refer to the covenant with Noah. But it is better to see—as we have seen above—these parts of the Noahic covenant as a republication of the creation covenant, for the later (Noahic) is derived from the former (creation), and the angels clearly fell before the Flood.

Similarly, Hosea says, "Like Adam, they have transgressed the covenant" (Hos 6:7). This verse is fraught with translation difficulties. Some think it refers to the rather obscure city of Adam and the inhabitants therein (Josh 3:16). Others think it refers to Adam the person. The best alternative may be a double entendre, where the person Adam comes to mind first, then the city of Adam comes to mind second. This has been argued convincingly by more than one person.[45] The point is, the Bible really does refer to an Adamic covenant prior to the Fall, a covenant that Adam broke.

At the heart of this covenant is Adam's (and his posterities'—see below) obligation to obey God. Adam's obedience was conditioned upon the commandment or law in much the same way that the ordinance/law is given to the rest of creation, including angels, to keep. All under the covenant were to "work" appropriately. When God tells Adam what he can do and not do, he is giving him a law to keep.[46] For this reason this covenant is sometimes called the *Covenant of Law* or *Covenant of Works*.

Covenant of Works in History

The Church Fathers recognized this covenantal relationship of Adam to God and His law. Irenaeus (c. 125-200 A.D.) says that God made a "covenant ... prior to the deluge, under Adam." He is not talking about Adam after the Fall, but prior to it. For, Adam "did not perform his commandment," and "the Lord did not abrogate the natural [precepts] of the law, by which man is justified, which also those who were justified by faith, and who pleased God, did observe previous to the giving of the law."[47] There is nothing after

---

[45] See Byron G. Curtis, "Hosea 6:7 and Covenant-Breaking like/at Adam," in *The Law is not of Faith*, ed. Bryan D. Estelle, J. V. Fesko, David Van Drunen (Phillipsburg, NJ: Presbyterian and Reformed, 2009), 170-209; Duane Garrett, *Hosea, Joel*, New American Commentary 19A (Nashville: Broadman and Holman, 1997), 162-63.

[46] God also gives other laws in Gen 1:28.

[47] Irenaeus, *Against Heresies* 3.11.8; 5.16.3; 4.13.1.

the Fall that tells us God gave him a specific commandment to obey or that he did or did not obey it. So Irenaeus has to be talking about a covenant made before Adam sinned.

Augustine also saw it. He says, "The first covenant, which was made with the first man, is just this: 'In the day you eat thereof, you shall surely die' … The covenant from the beginning is, 'You shall die the death.'"[48] I bring up these examples because seeing Adam under a covenant prior to the Fall is often said to be a novelty of the Reformed tradition, that no one prior to them understood Adam's relationship to be covenantal. This obviously overstates the case quite a bit.

Dealing with Objections

It is one thing for there to be a covenantal relationship; it is another for it to be a relationship based upon works. Many people smirk at the later, saying things like "God would never require that which he finds repulsive—to work for heaven," or "Father's won't make their sons work for their love." But the Covenant of Works does not teach that God is requiring Adam to "work for His love." Rather, it is working for a *reward*. His general love for his image bearers (which certainly includes the reprobate as noted above in the Covenant of Redemption) is unconditional. The reward is not. It is easy to think of instances where this could occur.

A son wants to go to college. The father loves his son, but he wants his son to appreciate his expensive education, so he conditions that he will help pay for it if the son also works to put himself through school. Does the father somehow hate

---

[48] Augustine, *City of God* 16:27.

his son because he puts this condition on him? Of course not. In fact, common sense viewing of the disaster which is our heartbreaking "culture of entitlement" teaches us that rather than a good thing, it is humiliating to have others pay for something you could pay for but refuse to. It is also disempowering. It is not a boost to self-esteem that losers get trophies "just for playing" or that students can get better grades by going to the teacher and asking them to raise the grade simply because they studied hard and did their best. Rather, it is only a boost to their narcissism. While it is now a badge of honor to be on welfare in many places, there used to be a great stigma attached to it, especially if you could work but wouldn't. Working to earn something is hardly a bad thing, even amongst such close kin as fathers and sons who love one another.

Of course, the analogy breaks down at some point. No good father will punish his son for not going to college because he wouldn't work for it. The "punishment" will be the son's future inability to get the kind of job he might otherwise be able to get. He will more than likely face some kind of consequences for his laziness. The covenant in Genesis 2 is different. God is testing his son Adam's fealty and obedience, but not threatening to withhold a Father's paternal love. We shouldn't try to make the analogy prove too much, but it is worth noticing that the punishment inflicted upon mankind in Romans 1 is actually the very sin we love most to commit. In other words, the analogy holds up to some degree even here, in that if the son refuses to go to college, he may face consequences of his own doing. He may not get a good job, be able to feed his family, etc. When God "gives us over," this *is* our punishment, seemingly both now and in eternity.

Rarely do we think of hell as the very thing that people want to go to, but that seems to be the idea of temporal "giving over" in Romans 1. So why not also an eternal giving over where the sin and its consequences are the punishment? People hate God, love their sin, and do not hate its consequences enough to stop sinning. God is giving us exactly what we want.

The idea of a works covenant is that it is the opposite of grace. One of the more common mistakes people make is that they merge the two ideas, finding grace in works and works in grace. Obtaining this reward in the Garden was not based on faith in Christ, but on obedience to the commandments of God (Christ). This does not imply that the obedience is done out of begrudging obligation; it is merely to say that faith is not the basis of the reward. Works is. It is outward, public, objective. If you obey, you will live; if you transgress, you will die. This is fair. This covenant is full of justice and goodness. We have seen that this is the exact principle found in Genesis 2-3. There is not a hint of grace found before the Fall. Indeed, why should there be? What sense does grace even make to a person holy and upright, having never sinned in any way, created in God's image and called his son? Why would God need to show grace to someone like that? Grace almost always implies that there is something wrong.

Works is in fact a principle found throughout the Scripture. Let's let the Scripture define what it means. In language that deliberately echoes Genesis 2, God tells Israel, "You shall therefore <u>keep</u> my statutes and my rules; if a person <u>does</u> them, he shall live by them: I am the LORD" (Lev 18:5; cf. Rom 10:5; Gal 3:12). Again, "If you faithfully <u>obey</u> the voice of the LORD your God, being careful to <u>do</u> all his commandments that I command you today, the LORD your God will set you <u>high above</u> all the nations of the earth" (Deut 28:1). This is a promise to return spiritually to the pristine heights of Mt. Eden (Ezek 28:14, 16), from which Adam was thrust. Again, "If you <u>walk</u> in my statutes and <u>observe</u> my commandments and <u>do</u> them, then I will give you rains in their season ... increase ... fruit ... harvest ... sowing ... bread ... and dwell in your land securely" (Lev 26:3-5). But, "If you forget the LORD your God and go after other gods and serve them and worship them, I solemnly warn you today that you shall surely perish ... because <u>you would not obey</u> the voice of the LORD your God" (Deut 8:19-20). Thus, when we talk about "works" we are talking about keeping, obeying, walking, observing, and doing all the law of God, turning neither to the right nor the left.

Romans 2 sums it up, "He [God] will render to each one according to his works: to those who by patience in well-doing seek for glory and honor and immortality, he will give eternal life; but for those who are self-seeking and do not obey the truth, but obey unrighteousness, there will be wrath and fury. There will be tribulation and distress for every human being who does evil, the Jew first and also the Greek, but glory and honor and peace for everyone who does good, the Jew first and also the Greek. For God shows no partiality" (Rom 2:6-11).

As Irenaeus said, this principle is not abrogated at the coming of Jesus Christ. Rather, it remains in place objectively in the world until Christ returns as a chief means of holding it accountable to God's moral commandments. It remains in place subjectively for salvation in an individual's life until that person *comes to* Christ. It even remains after a person comes to Christ, except now, rather than earning a reward, obedience is rendered out of thankfulness for the reward which has already been given through Christ's obedience and faith in him. This is most certainly the way the law will continue to work in eternity future, where those saved by grace and freed from sin will want to obey God, while those left in sin and to their own devices will only increase their hatred and disobedience to God—forever.

How this works goes back to Adam in the Garden. Adam represented all humanity. Like the kings of Israel after him, as he goes, so they go. If the king does well, the people prosper. If the king disobeys, the people suffer. This is not karma, but representation, where one person stands up (or falls down) for others. The Apostle explains this no less than five different ways in five verses, just so we'll get the point.

- Many died through one man's trespass. (Rom 5:15)
- The judgment following one trespass brought condemnation. (Rom 5:16)
- Because of one man's trespass, death reigned through that one man. (Rom 5:17)
- One trespass led to condemnation for all men. (Rom 5:18)
- By the one man's disobedience the many were made sinners. (Rom 5:19)

Notice the language in the last verse: Disobedience. Its opposite is "obedience." A perfectly good synonym for obedience is "works." And this word "works" is contrasted with "grace" in other places (Rom 11:6; Gal 3:2; Eph 2:8-9; 2 Tim 1:9), even as disobedience is contrasted with grace and "the gift" here (see Rom 5:17).

Let's return to Romans 2 for a moment. When Paul says that God will give to each person according to what he has done, several things should be observed. First, notice the conditions. You have to—with *all* your might—seek glory, honor, and immorality. You cannot, in any way, be self-seeking, disobey the truth, and obey unrighteousness. To put it another way, you have to be perfect. Perfection is the condition, not approximation or sincerity or trying hard.

Perfection is necessary because God is perfect. Thus, the Law says, "You shall be holy, for I the LORD your God am holy" (Lev 19:2). Anyone who knows what God is actually like will see just how holy that is, but just in case they miss it Jesus gives the full meaning (rather than a new law or new meaning), "You therefore must be perfect, as your heavenly Father is perfect" (Matt 5:48). In the churches I grew up in we sang the song, "I Surrender All." I always wondered to myself, "Do these people really believe they are doing that? It seems pretty impossible to me." I've never liked that song. But that's the idea.

The second thing to notice is that this little passage in Romans comes right in the middle of two full chapters of Paul proving that *no one is* like this. All people break the law (Rom 1:18-2:5; 12-13; 3:9-20). Gentiles have the "work of the law" written on their hearts and have consciences that accuse and defend them, because they disobey that law (Rom 2:14-16). Jews have the law on tablets, break the law, and cause Gentiles to blaspheme God (Rom 2:17-27).

The third thing to notice is that everyone, whether they have the Mosaic Law written on stones or the law written on their heart of stone (in both cases the moral part of the law is identical), has a covenantal relationship with God, and this includes after Jesus died. People are fond of saying, "You need to have a personal relationship with Jesus Christ." According to the Bible, everyone already does. Remember, a covenant is defined first and foremost as a relationship. The problem is, it is a relationship built now on treachery and lies. So Paul says, "Although they knew God, they did not honor him as God or give thanks to him, but they became futile in their thinking, and their foolish hearts were darkened" (Rom 1:21). It is not merely that they knew "about" God, but that they *knew* God. This is not pure head knowledge, as if they only know that God exists. It is relational knowledge. To know God is to have a relationship with him.

This relationship is defined by this covenant with Adam—this Covenant of Works and obedience to that which they know he requires, because it is written on their heart. It is imperative to understand this, for it is this covenantal relationship that all human beings have with God that makes them accountable to him. There is no one who can say, "But you didn't reveal yourself to me. I didn't know you. I didn't know what you wanted from me." Let us remember that when God wrote that law on stones it was called the tablets of the covenant (Deut 9:9, 11). Therefore, to have the law written on a heart of stone (Ezek 36:26; Rom 2:15) is to be a living tablet of the covenant. Each time we sin we become a walking, breathing legal and relational contradiction. This Covenant of Works therefore runs through the entire history of the present age.

But who will stand and who will fall? If everyone is under a Covenant of Works and everyone breaks it, who can be saved? Who can be redeemed? There is no greater question that can be asked. Usually, people will only ask it once they come to the end of themselves. That is what the Covenant of Works is meant to do. It is meant to humble us and to prepare us for good news. To begin to answer this question, we turn to the next kind of covenantal structures in Scripture.

Gracious Legal Covenants

Preliminary Observations and Problems

WE ARE GOING TO BEGIN LOOKING into the relationship of grace to the post-Fall covenants. It is tempting to begin this chapter the way we have the previous two, with stories and passages from the Bible. I would rather let the Bible do the talking first. But we need to start by saying something about the system of covenant theology, especially for those already familiar with the system.

The most popular way of thinking about post-Fall covenants from the perspective of covenant theology is to refer to them all as the "Covenant of Grace." This is certainly how I cut my teeth on the system. However, this has never been the *only* way of thinking about them. "Covenant of Grace" is not a biblical expression. It is a theological idiom, created for a system. But systems are fluid and fungible, man-made and prone to interpretation and revision. There is no agreement on what covenants belong in Covenant of Grace. Why?

As we just said, many people equate any or every OT covenant between God and man—and there are several (after the Covenant of Works)—with or within (depending upon who is in mind) the Covenant of Grace, as if they were all identical. Someone says, "The Abrahamic Covenant? Oh, that's the Covenant of Grace." Strangely, as we will see, though this is a basic default position for many, it is not consistently applied to every OT gracious covenant.[49] Questions often arise about the legal aspect, perhaps even the basic structure, of these some of these covenants, especially the Mosaic covenant. Is that the Covenant of Grace too? It seems so ... *legal*; therefore, it must be something like a republication of the Covenant of Works. (Of course, there are also laws in the Abrahamic covenant, but few will say this about Abraham's covenant). And then what happens when we get to the NT? What happens when the new covenant arrives on the scene and supersedes the old covenant so that we are "not under law, but under grace" (Rom 6:14-15), having made the first covenant obsolete (Heb 8:13)? Is the Covenant of Grace somehow overthrowing the Covenant of Grace? Is it overthrowing the Covenant of Works? What would be the implications of these things? Would it mean that God doesn't care if we obey the law anymore? Or, how could there be *anything* legal about the new covenant if the old has been thrown away? Thus, we can start to see the difficulties.

One last complication to consider arises when we come to realize that the Covenant of Grace, however it is understood, is often filtered by one's view of baptism. In fact, this is very much a chicken and egg question, and it is difficult to actually know which view drives the other. Someone says, "What does baptism have to do with anything?" The answer is, potentially, everything.

It is covenant theology that has been responsible in large part for the theological justification that infants are supposed

---

[49] I'm referring specifically to the Levitical Covenant (see the chapter on the Levitical Covenant below).

to be baptized. This is true in Presbyterian, Anglican, and Roman Catholic theology. But do they even agree amongst themselves on how to formulate their covenant theology? Furthermore, Reformed Baptists have developed a covenant theology that does not lead to infant baptism. This is so startling to many infant Baptists that they will put "Reformed" in quotes when speaking to (and rolling their eyes at) Reformed Baptists. So which version do we buy into?

Such difficulties create a minefield of interpretive hazards. There are pitfalls, but if we are careful in our inquiry, we can also navigate safely through them. In what follows, I will present a Reformed Baptist view of covenant theology that emphasizes both the unity and discontinuity of the various OT covenants to the new covenant. Unity and discontinuity is something all covenant theologians have, but the emphasis of one over the other sometimes differs. Let us begin by thinking about the unity or continuity.

Aspects of Continuity

As I have argued, continuity is the more basic component of a good covenant theology. How does Scripture present the continuity of the covenants to us? In what follows, we will look at several points: promises, the seed, typology, law, and grace. We will begin with promises.

Promises

It refers to the many covenants in the OT by the same term: "covenants of promise" (Eph 2:12). Notice the plural. I will argue that all OT covenants contain promises, not just some. These promises exude grace rather than law or works. For that reason, they can be viewed as *gracious covenants*. In the new covenant, these covenants of promise find their fulfillment. So promise-fulfillment is an idea that brings them all together, thus giving them a basic unity.

The Seed

The central promise common to OT covenants is that of a coming *seed*. In the midst of God's righteous judgment upon Satan, Eve, and Adam (which we will look at below), something unexpected occurs. The curse becomes a blessing and a promise for our first parents. The passage is famous, "I will put enmity between you and the woman, and between your <u>offspring</u> (seed) and her <u>offspring</u> (seed); he shall bruise your head, and you shall bruise his heel" (Gen 3:15). The idea of the "seed" found in this oath ties all of the OT covenants of promise together along with the new covenant in an explicit way.

The "seed" makes sense of the unity of the OT covenants. Besides Adam and Eve, God gives the promise to Noah and his seed (Gen 9:9). This promise is then funneled down through Abraham and his seed (Gen 12:7; 17:7), Isaac and his seed (Gen 26:3), Jacob and his seed (Gen 28:13; Num 24:7), and Judah and his seed.[50] The seed promises to the Patriarchs are then carried forward through Moses (Deut 1:8; 10:15), Aaron and his seed (Ex 28:43; Num 25:13), and David and his seed (2 Sam 7:12; Ps 89:5, 30, 37). The language in each

---

[50] Gen 38 and the bizarre story of Judah's wicked son spilling his seed must be read through the promise coming through Judah; cf. Ruth 4:12.

instance is almost identical, thus creating a deep and profound harmony among the covenants.

Near Seed Fulfillments

Now, each of these "seed" promises are fulfilled in both
the near and far future. This also creates unity. The near-
future fulfillments (all still within the vistas of the OT landscape) help weave individual OT covenantal threads together
into a single grand tapestry. This tapestry, fully formed, creates an image—a picture of something to come. This image is
then linked to the far-off fulfillment that comes in the NT
era and through Jesus Christ.

For example, the OT promise to make Abram into a
great nation is a physical-biological promise. This promise is
wrapped up with the doctrine of election (both corporate and
individual). Election has to do with God choosing something
ahead of time simply because it pleases him to do so. Because
of this, we do not understand this promise to arise out of thin
air with Abram as if God were doing something capriciously.
Rather, previous covenants link us to this promise.

This is usually seen via genealogies. So the covenantal
promise given to Adam comes to Noah, who comes from his
lineage (Gen 6:18; 9:9).[51] Then it comes to Shem (Gen 9:26),
the son of Noah. Abram is chosen from this line (Gen 11:10-
26). Each was given the covenant promise. It is no accident
that God chooses Abram rather than someone from, say, the

---

[51] See the genealogy of Genesis 5. For more on the covenants with Adam and Noah, see
below.

ancient lands of Scandinavia, for they are descended from the wrong son of Noah.

It is out of this covenantal link that God comes to Abram with a covenant (Gen 15:18; 17:2ff.). Then, showing God's purposes in election, it goes to Isaac (rather than Ishmael who was the oldest; Gen 17:21), then to Jacob (not Esau; Ex 2:24). Jacob then becomes Israel, God's chosen nation (Deut 7:6). In this way, God fulfills the temporal-physical promise to create a nation out of the nations (Gen 12:2).

This temporal, physical nation is given temporal-physical promises at this time. These come through three typological OT covenants made with Moses (the great prophet), Levi (the priest), and David (the king).

These were all present in an incipient form with Abraham. There was the promise of a specific <u>plot of land</u> that would be inherited (Gen 12:7). This is fulfilled through the covenants made with Moses (Deut 4:13-14) and Joshua (Josh 23:16), thus linking them together with Abraham (Deut 1:8; Josh 24:2).

There is the promise of <u>a king</u> who would sit on a throne (Gen 17:6; 35:11; 49:10; Num 24:17). This is fulfilled in David, and then through his sons (1 Kgs 1:13, 17; Ps 89:27-29). Yet, it too originates earlier, in Judah (Gen 49:10-11) and Jacob (Num 24:17). Hence, more unity.

Finally, there is the promise of <u>a priesthood</u>.[52] This is fulfilled in Aaron and his descendants (Ex 28:42; Num

---

[52] This is implicit in Melchizedek (Gen 14:18), which Hebrews then compares the Aaronic priesthood to (Heb 7:5-9, 11). It is implicit in Levi in the scattering promise given to him by Jacob (Gen 49:7) because of his actions, which are very similar to Phinehas' who receives the narrowed covenant promise (compare Gen 34:22 and Num 25:1-13). It is

18:19-26; Num 25:12-13; Deut 18:1-2; 1 Kgs 2:35; Ezek 48:11), but originates with Levi (Mal 2:4) and, eternally speaking, in Melchizedek (Ps 110:4). As we have seen, these offices of prophet, priest, and king were originally held by Adam in the Garden of Eden. Thus, through the promise-fulfillment of OT covenantal unity, temporal-physical promises were kept.

Far Seed Fulfillments

With these promises, however, God also signals his purpose to overcome our sin and rebellion through the glorious coming work of Christ. None of these near seeds were perfect; each was sinful and failed miserably. Christ is the one who is the Ultimate Seed (Gal 3:16). Jesus is the far-fulfillment of these various "seed" promises; he is the Prophet, Priest, and King.[53] We will develop these much more once we move into the specific covenants.

Jesus does this through something called the "new covenant" (Jer 31:31; Luke 22:20; 1 Cor 11:25; 2 Cor 3:6; Heb 8:8, 13; 9:15; 12:24). Through him, the complete fulfillment of the OT covenantal promises is achieved. This takes place in three stages. *First*, they are fulfilled in the physical-literal

---

implicit in the sacrifice that Abraham is to offer up to God (Gen 22; cf. 3:21; 4:1-5; 8:20-21). It is explicit in Jewish literature before the time of Christ where they said that Levi was given a covenant (Jubilees 30:18; 31:11-15). It becomes more explicit in the Bible in Aaron (Ex 28:43). Finally, it is absolutely clear in Phinehas (Num 25:12-13).

[53] These offices become increasingly differentiated as redemptive history progresses, so that by the time of 2 Kings, you find all three in the same verse, "The king went up to the house of the LORD, and with him all the men of Judah and all the inhabitants of Jerusalem and the priests and the prophets, all the people, both small and great. And he read in their hearing all the words of the Book of the Covenant that had been found in the house of the LORD" (2 Kgs 23:2).

person and work of Jesus Christ in his First Coming. *Second*, they are fulfilled spiritually in the church, through a spiritual children (sons of God), a heavenly kingdom, a spiritual temple, eternal life, and so on, after Jesus rises from the dead, ascends into heaven, and sends the Holy Spirit. *Finally*, at the end of the age, at the time of the Second Coming, the spiritual and physical promises will kiss, and God will unite the two into one, making a new heavens, a new earth, and giving us new resurrected bodies. Covenant theology does not "spiritualize" everything as is often claimed. But it makes the proper distinctions at the proper time between the physical and the spiritual realities of the present age and the age to come.

Typology

The covenantal promises between the OT and NT are also united together by something called typology. This is a word that signifies both sameness and difference (see below), unity and diversity. Typology is a NT word (Rom 5:14; 1 Cor 10:6; Heb 8:5; etc.), used to explain the redemptive-historical relationship between persons, places, events, actions or things, especially from OT to NT. This kind of relationship exists for example between Noah and Christ or Abraham and Christ, or between the Promised Land of Israel and the Kingdom of God, or the biological children of Abraham and the sons of God. The former relates organically to the later: person to person, place to place, thing to thing.

The relationship is similar to something like the image of Abraham Lincoln on a penny to the actual man. In fact, the image on the penny is literally stamped ("typed") onto the blank metallic planchet. Types are meant to point to something greater than themselves. So Jesus is called the greater Solomon (Matt 12:42), or the last Adam (1 Cor 14:45), his body is the Temple of God (John 2:21), he was the Rock that followed Israel in the wilderness (1 Cor 10:4), and so on.

Law

Two last points of unity must not be missed between OT and NT covenants. The first is the idea of law. There is law in *all* biblical covenants. This does not make them all covenants of works, however. Law is found throughout Scripture. For now, all we mean by "law" is a command that God issues that people must obey. These laws can be positive in nature ("be fruitful and multiply" in Gen 1:28 or "believe on the Lord Jesus Christ and you will be saved" in Acts 16:31) or negative ("you shall <u>not</u> murder" in Ex 20:13 or "do <u>not</u> neglect to show hospitality to strangers" in Heb 13:2).

Generally speaking, laws come in the verbal form known as the imperative mood. The imperative mood commands or requests, it gives prohibition or permission. It is found everywhere throughout the Bible in both Testaments.

Covenant theology recognizes the category of "moral law." Moral law is transcendent, transcultural, and timeless. It is always morally reprehensible everywhere and in all places to torture little babies for fun, or to steal another man's wife, or to worship a god other than the Creator. These laws reflect the eternal, unchanging moral nature of God himself.

The same moral law is found in all covenants. It was wrong for Cain to murder Abel (Gen 4:8), it was wrong for

Levi and Simeon to murder the town of Shechem (Gen 34:25-26), it was forbidden for Israel to kill unlawfully in the sixth commandment (Ex 20:13; Deut 5:17), it was wrong for David to kill his friend Uriah (2 Sam 11:15-17), and it is still forbidden and wrong to do this today (Matt 7:21; James 2:11; 4:2; 1 John 3:12). Importantly, the "wrongness" has *always included* the internal condition of the heart called by older theologians, a "hatred of abomination"—a hatred that seeks the worst of its fellow man.[54] It isn't like it suddenly became wrong to hate in this way when Jesus gave his Sermon on the Mount.

Grace

A final point of unity in all of these post-Fall covenants is the idea of grace. In fact, because they all have grace in them, the term Covenant of Grace has been used, mostly by Paedobaptists, to refer to all of them together. Many Reformed Baptists believe it is an error to call the OT covenants of promise "The Covenant of Grace," even though they are all gracious in some respects. Grace does tie them all together, but there are also differences that need to be pointed out here. It is to these that I will now turn.

Aspects of Discontinuity

Even as I have talked about the continuity between the covenants through such things as the seed, the promises, ty-

---

[54] Gen 37:5; Lev 19:17. There is a righteous hatred that is possible to have, as well as kinds of killing that do not violate the sixth commandment. This is made clear when God himself is said to hate something or when he commands certain kinds of killing.

pology, law, and grace, so also I must point out the important differences between the covenants, especially between the various old covenants and the new covenant.

The Seed

We'll start with the seed. The main point to make here is that Christ is not Adam. He is not Noah or Abraham or any of the other OT seeds. Again, there is continuity with them and this can be seen especially in his biological lineage through Mary and via adoption through Joseph. Jesus was fully man. But there is also profound discontinuity which can be viewed especially through his heavenly Father. Jesus is not *merely* a man. Though fully man, he is also fully God, and this creates discontinuity between all of the covenants of promise and the new covenant. Their covenant heads at an essential point are fundamentally different.

The Promises

Next come the promises. The biggest difference here is that temporary fulfillments turn into eternal fulfillments. King David was the near fulfillment of the kingship. Jesus is the far fulfillment, and the eternal one. Since Jesus is not merely a man, his kingship is different in that it is everlasting. All "everlasting" covenants from the OT are everlasting precisely because they find their fulfillment in Christ.

The near fulfillment of the Promised Land involves a very specific set of geographic coordinates, land features, mountains, and cities. The far fulfillment is a spiritual kingdom that will, even farther away still, become physical in the new earth that children of Abraham inherit (Matt 5:5; Rom 4:13). Do not mistake "spiritual" for "fake." Heaven is a real place; it just isn't physical in the way earth is physical.

Covenant theology takes things in the new covenant quite physically. The nation of Israel is a specific biological race of human beings. It always will be. But "true Jews" (Rom 2:28-29; 9:6; etc.), "the Israel of God" (Gal 6:16) are born of the spirit rather than the flesh (Gal 4:27-29). We can see in these things that there is also a difference between that which is physically temporary and that which is eternally spiritual. Sometimes the spiritual becomes physical in the future (the new earth), sometimes it does not (the temple in heaven).

Typology

Again we turn to typology to help clarify this point. Typology points to both continuity and *discontinuity* (Abraham Lincoln is not actually on a penny, his image is). In the new covenant as it has been inaugurated today, there is not total fulfillment in every respect, as the NT still sees an already/not-yet distinction between the present and the future. Nevertheless, the promise of the Coming Seed has been fulfilled once and for all. This includes many things that he brought with his coming that are related to the OT's types and shadows.

Christ's kingdom—the kingdom of God—is not the physical nation of Israel, nor is the church the physical nation of Israel (no one has ever said that it is). Christ's children are not biologically descended from him. His covenant is not a covenant of promises in the same way that all the others were; for he fulfills those promises in his active and passive obedience to the Father, and makes salvation through grace alone by the Holy Spirit possible. But each is related via typology, which expresses both similarity and difference.

Law

Next, we return to the idea of law. While it is true that law is found in all covenants, it is not true that it functions *the same way* in all covenants. In fact, it is my contention that two different people can actually approach *the same covenant* in two different ways and, theoretically, both could obtain the blessing. This is critical and fundamental to understanding covenant theology, and not a few have been profoundly confused by this point.

Sometimes law (i.e. commands) forms <u>the basis</u> of obtaining blessings or curses. We have seen just this from numerous passages in our look at the Covenant of Works. Many national, physical OT promises were obtained the same way, especially (but not exclusively) under the Mosaic covenant. In other words, a person could approach the covenant with Moses *as if it were* a covenant of works. If so, the law then gives the conditions for meeting the terms of that covenant and obtaining the blessings in that way. The condition is perfect obedience.

Anyone living in the OT under a covenant theoretically could have approached the covenant in this way and been justified. This is because God was still looking for his new Adam, his perfect representative that would keep his law and the offices of prophet, priest, and king perfectly. It is also because God is fair (Rom 2:11). He will give to each person according to what he has done. To those who by persistence seek glory, honor and immorality he will give eternal life (Rom 2:7). At any given time in the OT, the law still needed to be obeyed. Noah is set up as a new Adam. Israel is created to be a new Adam. Any Israelite—especially one of its covenantal heads—could have (theoretically) fulfilled the seed promise and ushered in eternal life.

However, one must never approach the new covenant in this way. Because to do so is to trample the son of God under foot (Heb 10:29, notice the Genesis 3:15 imagery here). This is to consider that which is perfectly clean, unclean. It is to say that no one has yet obeyed the law (cf. Heb 4:15) as the second Adam. Therefore, someone must still arise to do so. There is no possibility of salvation for such as this, because they are sinful themselves and have despised the only hope of obtaining mercy.

Grace

As soon as a person in the OT recognized their failure to keep the law, they were obligated to change their stance towards the covenant from one of works to one of grace. God would be merciful under any OT covenant, even regarding temporary, physical, temporal blessings, *if* they repented and sought the Lord's favor by grace.[55] This was especially true regarding the promise of eternal salvation. Thus, *the very same*

---

[55] There is a difficult question here of God not giving temporal blessings, even when a person did repent. One thinks of Moses who was not allowed to enter the Promised Land. Grace does not oblige God to give sinners all of the promises, because they have, in fact, broken the law. Also, many times these things were done in biblical redemptive history to teach lessons or to usher in a new covenantal epoch, such as the coming of Christ.

covenant could also be approached as if it were a gracious covenant, indeed, as if it were the Covenant of Grace (though it was, in fact, not; see below), its blessings dependent upon God's grace and forgiveness. This is true in any OT covenant.

What is grace? It is popularly thought that grace is "unmerited favor." While this is true, the Bible almost always uses the term with regard to sinners.[56] For this reason, some have talked about grace as "*de*merited favor." God does not merely send grace to neutral people; he sends it to sinners who have actually *merited* wrath. "The *wages* of sin is death" (Rom 6:23; cf. Prov 10:16). A wage is what you earn, what you merit. Spoken of in this way, prior to the entrance of sin through the violation of the command in the Garden of Eden, there was no demerit, and therefore, there was no need for God to show grace. The covenant prior to the Fall extended a benefit to Adam on the basis of what he did. There was no grace involved, nor, again, does there need to be. Grace in this sense is simply a non-issue. After the Fall, however, it is a different matter.

As we think about post-Fall covenants, it is important to emphasize that in each of them, God is the one who comes to the man. Because man is a sinner, this must be considered some kind of an act of grace up front. Thus, each OT covenant would have this as a point of continuity. Consider Noah. It was the promise that came first: God would save him and his family through the flood (Gen 6:13-21). He found grace (favor) in the eyes of the LORD (6:8).

---

[56] The exception is Jesus who found grace/favor (*charis*) with God (Luke 2:40). Clearly, "grace" is not being used in this way here.

It is into this grace that the command to "build the ark" comes. Noah obeyed God, but not in order to merit his favor. He already had it. Therefore, in this case, obedience to the law is the result of having already obtained a spiritual gracious and unconditional blessing from God. Noah built his ark "by faith" (Heb 11:7). In this way, Noah's obedience saved him from the waters of the flood. It was a temporal, temporary blessing that pointed towards a spiritual, eternal reality (1 Pet 3:20-21).

This idea of grace is present in all OT covenants, including Moses. "God merciful and gracious, slow to anger, and abounding in steadfast love and faithfulness" (Ex 34:6, RSV). Even the Ten Commandments begin with grace, "I am the LORD your God who brought you out of the land of Egypt" (Ex 20:2). "The gift of God is expressed in his actions of extending mercy, loving-kindness, and salvation to people."[57]

But God's grace cannot just be divvied out willy-nilly, because God "feels" like it. Rather, the law still must be upheld. Thus, when we come to the new covenant, we see that a man who already had God's favor, yet had done no wrong, ends up obeying the law perfectly in every way, as prophet, priest, and king. Thus, The Covenant of Grace made with Christ differs greatly from any OT covenant, for it is what they all pointed toward, even as he is the one the covenant people of God pointed towards and were to look to for salvation. It is the substance; they are the shadow. Thus, is it for

---

[57] Walter A. Elwell and Philip Wesley Comfort, *Tyndale Bible Dictionary*, Tyndale Reference Library (Wheaton, IL: Tyndale House Publishers, 2001), 550.

our failures and sins that we read, "Grace and truth came through Jesus Christ" (John 1:14).

Covenantal Relationships

I now want to turn your thoughts to looking more directly at how the covenants relate to one another. I have demonstrated similarities and differences. So now, how do we fit it all together? What is the relationship between the "covenants of promise" and the new covenant? How we parse this will make all the difference in the world. But however we do it, we must make sense of both the continuity and the discontinuity between them all—especially as they relate to the new covenant.

Defining "The Covenant of Grace"

Perhaps the place to start is with defining the Covenant of Grace. Again, when infant Baptists speak of the Covenant of Grace, they usually mean each and every one of these covenants taken individually and/or collectively (perhaps minus Moses). Thus, each (post-Fall) covenant is an "administration" of the one Covenant of Grace. The Abrahamic covenant is the Covenant of Grace, the Noahic Covenant is the Covenant of Grace, etc. This is a bit simplistic, since they too want to make sense of differences. However, at the key point, which is the relationship of the new covenant to the covenants of promise, they identify such covenants as Abraham and Christ as both being The Covenant of Grace.

Reformed Baptists believe this is a mistake. While maintaining continuity, this does not take into account—

enough—the discontinuity. Jesus is not Abraham. Thus, Reformed Baptists, while agreeing that there is grace in covenants of promise—grace that is sent prospectively, in anticipation of the Covenant of Grace—nevertheless define "The Covenant of Grace" as the new covenant made with Christ. So we can think of the Covenant of Grace as "the gracious plan of salvation that God has given us in Christ."[58] Old covenants are gracious. Old covenants typify Christ. But they are not the Covenant of Grace anymore than Christ is literally a lamb. He is a lamb, but he is not an animal.

Thus, we are making a distinction between the phrase with capital letters and the same phrase without them:

covenants of grace ⟶ gracious aspects of OT covenants which prefigure the Covenant of Grace

Covenant of Grace ⟶ the new covenant

An Analogy

There is a simple analogy I like to use to help people understand this continuity and discontinuity between the covenants. It is an analogy, so it is not meant to be taken beyond its purpose. It is the analogy of the creation week. The "week" creates the unity in the analogy. God created the earth in six days. On the seventh day he rested (Ex 20:11). The "days" create the discontinuity or difference.

---

[58] This is a quote from Morton Smith as brought to my attention by Dr. Robert Gonzales. Curiously, Smith is a Paedobaptist, but his definition comports with that of Reformed Baptists.

Each day was unique; God made something different on each day. But the seventh day was different from the others in a profound way, for on it God did not work. This is highlighted literarily by the lack of a "morning and evening" formula on the seventh day. Yet, together, these seven days comprise the creation week.

In many ways, the various OT covenants are portrayed as new creations,[59] so the analogy has some biblical support. The same is true with the new covenant. In fact, the first (symbolic) week of Jesus' earthly ministry is presented in John's Gospel as six creative days where the Lord "calls" his disciples to himself, followed by a seventh day feast (a new creation).[60]

Creation Week		Redemption (New Creation) Week	
Six Work Days	Day 1	Six OT Covenants	Adamic Covenant
	Day 2		Noahic Covenant
	Day 3		Abrahamic Covenant
	Day 4		Prophetic Covenant (Moses)
	Day 5		Priestly Covenant (Levi)
	Day 6		Kingly Covenant (David)
Day of Rest	Day 7	NT Covenant of Rest	New Covenant (Christ)

In the analogy, days are to a week what the covenants of promise and the Covenant of Grace are to redemptive history. In my understanding, there are six post-Fall OT covenants, each being made with a specific covenant head (Adam,

---

[59] I go into this in some detail in my book Waters of Creation: A Biblical-Theological Study of Baptism (Erie, CO: Waters of Creation Pub., 2009). That book deals to some degree with covenant theology, but the present volume gives my more mature reflections on this subject.
[60] Day 1: John 1:19-28; Day 2: vv. 29-34; Day 3: vv. 35-42; Day 4: vv. 43-51; Day 7: 2:1-11.

Noah, Abraham, Moses, Levi, David).[61] Sometimes, some of their specific sons are also included (Shem under Noah, Isaac and Jacob under Abraham, Solomon under David, etc.). There is one NT covenant—the new covenant. It is made with Jesus Christ. These six covenants climax in a new covenant wherein we enter God's rest (Heb 4) in a new creation (2 Cor 5:17; Gal 6:15). This rest is entered into "already," yet anticipates full realization in the Great Day, represented figuratively as the "first day" or "eighth day" in the Scripture. This is the eternal day that has begun to see the first light of dawn (Christ's defeat of death), but hasn't yet reached the glorious, eternally bright high noon (Rom 13:12).[62] We will speak about later.

The Covenant of Redemption

This analogy shows the relationship between old covenants and the new covenant. But what about the Covenant of Redemption? How does it fit into all of this? Let's look at grace to answer the question.

---

[61] Most systematic treatments deal only with five OT covenants, though not all. See for example Kevin J. Conner and Ken Malmin, *The Covenants: The Key to God's Relationship with Mankind* (Portland, OR: City Bible Publishing, 1997). It is important not to commit a Guilt by Association (Bad Company) fallacy here. Dispensationalism sees seven dispensations, and some might be tempted to say that it is wrong to see seven covenants because it seems Dispensational. But there is nothing inherently wrong with seven or six or five, and we are talking about covenants, not dispensations.

[62] The analogy is not intended to compare what God makes during the days of creation with what God does in each successive covenant. Though, two points can be made. First, as in the creation week, there is a progressive nature to the OT covenants. They build upon one another. Second, there may be some unintended overlaps such as the light and dark of day one contrasting with good and evil with Adam, the water of day two overlapping with Noah's flood, the land of day three overlapping with the promise of land to Abraham, and so on.

As we saw in the Covenant of Redemption, God's grace in Christ has ineffectual overtones that are meant to display God's kindness to the world (Rom 2:4), and to lead and call sinners to Christ (Matt 22:14; John 3:14-17; 12:32). We often speak of this ineffectual grace as *common grace*, though it is the very same grace that also saves people. This grace is "common" because it is given to all people. It is "ineffectual" because it is not effectually, savingly applied by the Holy Spirit in God's good pleasure. God sends it to all for non-salvific purposes such as displaying his kindness, benevolence, patience, and tolerance to the world. Nevertheless, it is deeply tied to covenants, as the story of Noah teaches us (Gen 9:8-17; cf. Heb 10:29). Common grace is extended in history, to people, via covenants. Thus, the Covenant of Redemption works its way out through common grace, and the temporary, temporal, physical blessings that are granted in the covenants.

Thankfully, grace also has effectual overtones through the invincible power of God and his sovereign will to draw and save to himself whomever he chooses by this grace (Matt 22:14; John 6:44). God is pleased to make this grace effectual through the Holy Spirit by combining it with the word (Word), specifically the proclamation of Jesus Christ crucified, raised, and ascended so that God might save us by his grace (Isa 52:7; Nahum 1:15; Acts 5:42; 8:12; 10:36; Rom 10:15; 16:25; 1 Cor 1:17; 2 Tim 2:8; 4:2; 1 Pet 1:12; etc.). By effectual, we mean that it actually brings those whom God has chosen to faith and salvation in his good timing (John 6:39; 17:12). Through the Spirit, it regenerates people. In fact, this is the only hope sinners—all of whom hate God and run from him (John 3:19-20; Rom 3:9-18) like a thief runs from the police—have. If God did not effectually apply grace in this way, none would be saved. This is what we often refer to as *special* or *saving grace*. Again, not that it is different grace, but that God's purposes in it are different. Thus, this grace that we discussed in the Covenant of Redemption is also closely tied to OT covenants (cf. Ps 25:12-16; 111:4-9), especially through the Covenant of Grace (Eph 2:8-13; Heb 13:20-25).

The Covenant of Works

We have seen that these old covenants are related in some way to the Covenant of Works. Now, let's make this more concrete. Whereas God originally set Adam in the Garden to earn the reward for himself and his posterity, so also he does for all those under OT covenants. But as we have seen, they all failed. But "at just the right time" (Gal 4:4), God sent forth his Son born of a woman under the law.

Christ earned his reward by obeying his Father in all he is sent to do "under the law" (Gal 4:4), or to put it another way, under the Covenant of Works. But his purpose in doing this was to extend the reward of life that he earned to all those who trust in him by faith alone. In other words, while he earned the reward, he now offers it (i.e. eternal life, the inheritance, sonship, salvation, etc.) as a gift to us. Thus, we receive it by faith through grace alone.

Thus, the Covenant of Grace is set at odds with the Covenant of Works. The Covenant of Grace is rooted in the Covenant of Works in that Christ obeys the later so that he may offer the gift through the former. But for us, they put forward opposite ways of attaining the reward, the inheritance, the prize, or the gift. This antithesis is put frankly in several places: "For the <u>law</u> was given through Moses; <u>grace</u> and truth came through Jesus Christ" (John 1:17). "It depends on faith [not law], in order that the promise may rest on grace and be guaranteed to all [Abraham's] seed" (Rom 4:16), and so on.

Final Thoughts

Grace is an idea that binds in some sense all historical covenants after the Fall. This helps us see the unity of God's plan of salvation. There is and always has been only one way that *fallen* people can inherit salvation. This comes by faith in Christ through grace alone. It always has and always will.

In the OT, salvation came through faith in the promises of Christ (cf. Heb 11:17), and in the Second Person of the Trinity whom they really knew, though not in human flesh. As it says, "[Moses] considered the reproach <u>of Christ</u> greater wealth than the treasures of Egypt, for he was looking to the reward" (Heb 11:26). "Your father Abraham rejoiced that he would see <u>my day</u>. He saw it and was glad" (John 8:56). "All drank the same spiritual drink. For they drank from the spiritual Rock that followed them, and <u>the Rock was Christ</u>" (1 Cor 10:4). "<u>Jesus</u>, who saved a people out of the land of Egypt, afterward destroyed those who did not believe" (Jude 5). In the NT, this comes through faith in the accomplished work of Christ come in the flesh, born under law.[63]

---

[63] This pervasive idea of Christ in the OT is vital to having a proper understanding of faith in Christ for OT saints. The NT gets this idea about Christ *from the OT* in many ways, but especially in the mysterious figure of the Angel of the LORD, who is the preincarnate Word of God. We will look at this a little later on.

In making the distinctions we have made here—seeing OT covenants as capable of being approached via works or grace, understanding that they are distinct yet related, each anticipating the new covenant, and so on, we are not stuck in our thinking about whether covenant x is "the Covenant of Grace" or "the Covenant of Works." We are able to approach each on its own terms, seeing both the unity with other covenants, and the distinct, individual contribution that each covenant makes in the history of redemption.

Gracious Legal Covenants: Adamic Covenant

WITH THESE INTRODUCTORY THOUGHTS out of the way, we are now ready to begin thinking about the various OT covenants. I begin with Adam. God made two covenants with our first parents. He made with them (specifically Adam) a Covenant of Works.[64] Afterwards, he made with them a gracious covenant. I have established the former and assumed the latter. Now let me establish it as well.

Adam and Eve

After Adam fell into sin, and Eve with him, the two (along with Satan, for it seems as we have shown that the angels were in some sense related to this covenant as well) were cursed and cast out from the presence of God, effectively "dying the death."[65] Yet, in the midst of this great punishment, God did something unexpected. The curse of Satan became a blessing and a promise for Eve. Blessings and promises are essential to covenants.

---

[64] This is why Adam rather than Eve (who sinned first) is the one through whom sin came. He parallels the Second Adam.

[65] That Satan effectively "dies" along with Adam and Eve is made clear by comparing Genesis 3:15 with Isaiah 14:12-15; Ezek 28:14-17; 31:3-17 (also Psalm 82) and recognizing that in the prophets, God uses the ancient Edenic symbols of the cosmic mountain and world tree to explain that behind the fall of a human nation (Babylon, Tyre, Assyria) is the fall/death of the evil supernatural Power that lies behind it.

The passage is famous, "I will put enmity between you and the woman, and between your offspring [seed] and her offspring [seed]; he shall bruise your head, and you shall bruise his heel" (Gen 3:15). This is the first declaration to humanity of the agreement made in eternity past in the Covenant of Redemption. It signals Christ's future work which will eventually fulfill the broken Covenant of Works. Likewise, it signals Christ's work that will eventually usher in the Covenant of Grace. And thus it says to us today, "The God of peace will soon <u>crush</u> Satan under your feet. The <u>grace</u> of our Lord Jesus Christ be with you" (Rom 16:20).

The covenantal context already established between God and Adam bears the hallmarks of a suzerain/vassal treaty. This promise bears the hallmarks of a covenant grant. One of our theologians has explained that "the royal grant assum[es] a suzerain-vassal relationship, which always requires loyalty ... it is the existing suzerain-vassal relationship that makes the royal grant a possibility."[66] It is because Adam was the son of God that God entered into this new arrangement with our forefather. What is unexpected is that royal grants are rarely given when the vassal or even the son is as treacherous as Adam was. But this is why it is called *gracious*.

Because of the guarantee sworn in the Covenant of Redemption, God was now free to enter into a different kind of covenant with humanity. The kind of covenant we have in mind here is a gracious covenant, though as we have discussed, it should not be confused with the Covenant of Grace

---

[66] Dr. Robert Gonzales Jr., "The Covenant Context of the Fall, Part 2: The Essence of a 'Covenant,'" http://drbobgonzales.com/2012/11/27/the-covenant-context-of-the-fall-part-2-the-essence-of-a-covenant/, last accessed 10-14-2014.

(capitalized for emphasis) properly speaking. It is this grace-principle that begins to be seen in Genesis 3:15 because of God's forbearance awaiting the finished, sacrificial work of Christ (Rom 3:25-26).

One of the vital elements of a covenant is that of a sacrifice. Formal covenants were said to be "cut." To "cut a covenant" is to enter into a covenant with blood. This covenant cutting was through the literal cutting of a sacrificial animal where the blood was poured out as an offering and the animal was often burned as a pleasing aroma or eaten as a covenant meal.

After our parents sinned, God came to them and questioned them. After blaming each other, God cursed them: Satan, Eve, then Adam. But he gave Eve that promise of the coming seed (as it was through Mary and not Joseph that Jesus would come). Then he did something even more unexpected. "And the LORD God made for Adam and for his wife garments of skins and clothed them" (Gen 3:21).

It isn't that God somehow created these skins out of thin air. These are animal skins. It is unthinkable that God took some dead animal that he found lying around and decided to turn that into a coat. No, this refers to a *sacrifice*. The LORD God, presumably in the form of the Angel of the Lord,[67] is actually present with them as he later will be with Abraham and others. He killed and sacrificed an animal, and graciously clothed our parents. This was the act of God; this was the act of Christ.

---

[67] I will not take the time to prove this here, since I will deal with this theme fairly extensively in the Covenant of Grace.

This sacrificing of an animal will soon be shown to be a profoundly covenantal act. In other words, we must view this act as being tied directly to a covenant "cutting." We will explore this idea below when we come to Noah, Abraham, and the priests. Regarding the priests, an ancient Jewish commentary (Targum) calls this clothing of Adam and Eve "a vesture of a priest"[68] (see Zech 3:1-5), meaning that God was declaring the couple holy, though they were not in fact holy. There was blood spilt here, and it is blood alone that is able to atone for their sin (Heb 10:4, 11).

However, this blood was not the blood of the sacrificial Lamb of God. It was merely an animal, and animal sacrifices are never able to *take away* sin. They can only cover it, as they look in anticipation to a greater, more perfect sacrifice to come. Therefore, the graciousness shown in this covenant was typological of the Covenant of Grace to come, the covenant that would be enacted only by the blood of Jesus.

This covenant was also retroactive. As Romans says, "In his divine forbearance, he passed over former sins" (Rom 3:25). Thus, because of what was coming, God could justify them and maintain his righteousness at the same time. This is the pattern set for all gracious OT covenants to come, and for this reason, we must never confuse these covenants with the Covenant of Grace, even if they happen to be gracious covenants from God. Animals are not Jesus.

Something else is shown here. Adam and Eve didn't do anything. They merely received the covering. We can be sure that they were thankful for it, and that they trusted this covering was better than their own "skins" of tree-leaves (Gen

---

[68] Targum Pseudo-Jonathan Genesis 3:21.

3:7). In this they foreshadow the faith that will soon be made apparent in the story of redemption.

Finally, and this is no small point, we should keep in mind here that God still punished our parents by tossing them out of the Garden of Eden. This covenant is gracious, but their own failed works must still be punished. There had to be repercussions for their violation of the previous covenant, even if this new-found gracious covenant would cover their previous transgressions. This shows the continuing nature of the Covenant of Works at this time, indeed even to our own time as all humans, even Christians, continue to die. Because we are Adam's children, we die (Gen 5; Rom 5:12-14). Blessed is he who only dies once (Rev 20:6).

Cain and Abel

This is further evidenced in the next story of Cain and Abel. The two brothers must offer the right and acceptable sacrifice or they will be consumed by sin and cursed. Sin crouches at the door like a demon,[69] but you must master it (Gen 4:7). There are two things to note here. First, they had to offer a sacrifice; it wasn't optional. This shows their present dirty condition and need to approach God in a specific way. This sacrifice had to be a bloody sacrifice, since it foreshadowed the sacrifice of the Lamb of God. They had to "do" the right thing themselves. This shows how they were still under a works principle.

---

[69] The term "crouching" (*rabats*) is actually a common term in the Ancient Near East for a demon. See the *Dictionary of Deities and Demons in the Bible*.

The second thing of note is that Abel offered his sacrifice by faith (Heb 11:4). This was in anticipation of the Greater Sacrifice to come (Heb 12:24). Abel seemed to understand this in some way. Thus, though they are still under a works principle in some sense (punishment, death), in as much as God looked favorably upon their sacrifice and their faith, they were under a grace principle which looked forward to the future. Both were true simultaneously, but not so as to merge or confuse the two ideas. Grace is not works. This correct parsing of the mixing of principles in the old covenant will be of no small help when we come to even more confusing covenants later on. They were to believe God by faith alone, and they were to offer the right sacrifice, in that order.

Gracious Legal Covenants: Noahic Covenant

THE FIRST MENTION OF THE WORD "covenant" (Hebrew: *berith*) is found in Genesis 6 with the story of Noah. It occurs both prior to and after the flood. "I will establish my covenant with you, and you shall come into the ark, you, your sons, your wife, and your sons' wives with you" (Gen 6:18). "I establish my covenant with you and your offspring after you" (Gen 9:9). As we can see, the language is virtually identical. However, the context of these passages is not identical.

Before the Flood

In the former, God is entering into a covenant with Noah to save Noah and his family from the Flood. There is a stipulation put upon Noah: He had to build an ark (Gen 6:14-16). If he did not build this ark, Noah, along with everyone else on earth, would die. However, Noah only built this ark because he believed God. "By faith Noah, being warned by God concerning events as yet unseen, in reverent fear constructed an ark for the saving of his household" (Heb 11:7). First Noah believed; then his faith was displayed in what he did. Notice the order and remember it.

As we learn elsewhere, this kind of faith is not the natural byproduct of a good person weighing his options in pristine righteous neutrality. Rather, this faith is the gift from God (Eph 2:8-9). This gift, once given, then begins to express itself in proper judgments, actions, and obedience. Think about it this way. If Noah really did believe God, then why *wouldn't he* have built this ark, no matter how difficult or impossible it may have seemed. What else was there to do?

Because of this faith and the saving nature of the covenant in Genesis 6 (he was saved through water), we rightly identify Noah here as the recipient of grace. Being saved from the flood in the ark is typological of being saved by Jesus Christ from the coming eternal wrath of God (1 Pet 3:19-21). Thus it says, "Noah found favor in the eyes of the LORD" (Gen 6:8). The word "favor" is better translated as "grace" (LXX, KJV). First he finds grace, then he is viewed as "righteous," "blameless,"[70] and walks with God (Gen 6:9). God saved Noah spiritually and then physically.

After the Flood

The second instance of "covenant" with Noah occurs after the flood, after Noah has been saved. Curiously—and this is important for enriching an understanding of the earliest biblical covenant—this covenant repeats ideas found not in Genesis 6, but in Genesis 1. "Be fruitful and multiply and fill the earth" (Gen 9:1; cf. 1:28). There are also references to the created animals,[71] the day and night,[72] the image of God,[73] and Noah's dominion.[74] In this way, Noah is a new Adam

---

[70] Technically the word "blameless" refers not to Noah's character, but to his function as an emissary for God or to his physically pure bloodline. See my discussion in my *Giants: Sons of the Gods*, 36-40.

[71] Compare Gen 8:17 and 1:22, 24.

[72] Compare Gen 8:22 and 1:5.

[73] Compare Gen 9:6 and 1:26-27.

[74] Compare Gen 9:2-5 and 1:26, 28.

starting on a new earth that was completely covered by water (see Gen 1:2).

Furthermore, we discover that the recipients of this post-Flood covenant include the earth and the animals and other things besides mankind (Gen 8:22; 9:12, 15). In other words, we seem to be returning to the covenant idea present prior to the Fall, prior to grace. This makes it clear that grace is now the necessary backdrop to carrying out these now otherwise unattainable covenant obligations. Since this covenant is mostly about physical salvation and blessing, it has been referred to as a covenant of common grace by some. Yet, it clearly harkens back to the covenant that came prior to the clothing of our parents; it speaks to the Covenant of Works-Life-Creation.

My conclusion therefore that it is sort of like Noah is being given the covenants in the reverse order that Adam received them. Adam began with works because he was created upright and holy; he finished with the promise of the future and subsequent grace so that he would not be destroyed. Noah begins with grace, for he is in the same condition as Adam after the Fall. But under this prescient gracious principle (anticipating the coming grace in Jesus Christ), Noah is reaffirmed in the covenant originally given to Adam. It had to be this way so that we would know that the Covenant of Works continues on as a vital idea throughout redemptive history. This will make much better sense when we look at how it is fulfilled by Christ in a later section.

This helps us see that grace absorbs the personal, legal basis for covenantal blessing upon perfection as it anticipates the coming Messiah. It then acts as the bubble around which "works" can be carried out faithfully. God is reestablishing

with mankind that he still expects man to carry out the covenantal obligations made with Adam in Eden, even though the
testing from a tree is no longer in place. Though, in this light,
it is extremely curious that Noah plants a vine-tree, finds
himself naked, and falls into sin immediately after getting off
the ark. There have been many who have seen more than one
connection between this story and the Fall of Adam.[75] Noah
is not Jesus Christ. He is flawed like his father Adam.

Yet, in the story and covenant of Noah, who will per-
form obedience? Those who find themselves in the grace of
God. Only by faith through grace can a person hope to please
God in the things that they do. This is the only way that
evangelical obedience is even possible. This is the meaning of
Noah's covenants.

---

[75] For more on this see my sermon "My Three Sons: New Adam, Same Result,"
http://www.rbcnc.com/Genesis%209.18-29%20My%20Three%20Sons%20New%20
Adam,%20Same%20Result.pdf, last accessed 10-14-2014.

Gracious Legal Covenants: Abrahamic Covenant

THE NEXT EXPLICIT MENTION OF "covenant" occurs in Genesis 15:18, "On that day the LORD made a covenant with Abram, saying, 'To your offspring I give this land.'" This covenant does not arise in a vacuum (anymore than it did with Noah). Like Noah who is connected to Adam through a genealogical line that teaches God's electing/preserving grace (Gen 5:1-32). Abram is connected to Noah through the faithful act and gracious promise of his ancestor—Shem.

Making a Name

Shem is one of three sons of Noah. After the flood waters abate, Noah plants a vineyard and gets drunk (Gen 9:20-21). His son Ham, being the youngest (Gen 9:22, 24), acts wickedly and, in my opinion, seeks to supplant the ordinary right of succession by having relations with Noah's wife.[76] This act was meant to publically humiliate his father and destroy his authority in the eyes of others, while simultaneously raising Ham to the status of patriarch via the child. The

---

[76] Ham "saw the nakedness" of Noah. This terminology is used elsewhere in Scripture to refer to a sexual act with a man's wife or other kin (cf. Lev 18:6-19; 20:11-21; Deut 22:30; 27:20; Ezek 22:10). This idea of nakedness also parallels the Adam and Eve story, though there is no hint of sexual impropriety in the biblical text there. See John Sietze Bergsma, "Noah's Nakedness and the Curse of Canaan (Gen 9:20-27)," *Journal of Biblical Literature* 124/1 (2005): 25-40.

product of this most unholy union was Ham's son Canaan. This is why Noah curses Canaan rather than Ham (Gen 9:25).

But Noah's other sons act righteously (Gen 9:23), and for this they are blessed (9:26-27). But the special blessing is reserved for Shem, through whom it is promised that redemption would one day come. "Shem" means "name" in Hebrew. There is a wordplay that will work through Shem, the Tower of Babel, and Abraham. Through Shem—Name—God will make a Name for himself (Gen 12:2), thus putting down the rebellion of mankind who wants to make a name for themselves (Gen 11:4). "Name" and "covenant" are related in many passages throughout the OT (cf. Deut 10:8; Ps 111:9; Jer 34:15; Mal 2:5).

Abraham

Abram is the man through whom the great promises of Christ and his Name would begin to be made known to a world now living in utter darkness, including Abram himself, for he and his father worshipped different gods than the LORD (Josh 24:2), and God came to Abram in an act of grace (Acts 7:2; cf. Gen 11:31-32). Thus, we get a genealogy that traces Abram back to Shem and Noah (11:10-27).

Before we even hear the word "covenant" with regard to Abram, we know that this man was chosen because of the promise and grace of God. When we come to the first recorded dialogue between the LORD and Abram, we find the LORD swearing an oath in a very one-sided way, much like a covenant grant. "I will make you into a great nation," "I will bless you and make your name great," I will bless those who bless you, and him who dishonors you I will curse," "In you all the families of the earth shall be blessed" (Gen 12:2-3). All there is for Abram to do is respond by faith. He must "go." "<u>Go</u> from your country and your kindred and your father's house to the land that I will show you" (12:1).

As with Noah and the ark, there is no reason Abram would have gone anywhere if he did not first believe God. And so his "going" was the product of his believing (Heb 11:8). If God will really do this, why wouldn't he go? When Abram gets to the land, God promises that he will inherit this land, as we have already seen. This land becomes typological of the whole earth in the Covenant of Grace that commences in Christ's death.

The next time the "covenant" is used, God promises Abram a son (Gen 17:16). The son and land combine in a remarkable way as Paul say, "For the promise to Abraham and his <u>offspring</u> that he would be heir of the <u>world</u>" (Rom 4:13). The boy Isaac would be typological of all those chosen by God and precious, heir of grace according to the promises of God and election (Rom 9:7-8). To prove it, God changes Abram's name to Abraham: The Father of Many Nations.

Again, it is important to not become confused on this point of typology, for here many have been snared in a web from which they cannot extricate themselves. God gave to Abram a gracious covenant, but it was not the Covenant of Grace, though it was treated by God because of his forbearance, as if it were. God was gracious to Abram and granted to him promises, promises that would eventuate themselves in the birth of The Son. These promises would be given spiritually to a spiritual people (Rom 4:16), of which Abraham was himself a member.

Along the way, this typological covenant, a very real, perfectly historical and physical covenant, was given to Abraham and his physical descendants that God was both gracious and righteous. Thus, the covenant or covenants (theologians disagree on whether God gave one or two different covenants to Abraham just as they do with Noah; I think there is only one) given to Abraham sometimes bear the marks of grants and sometimes bear the marks of suzerain treaties. Sometimes they appear utterly gracious; sometimes they appear as if works is the guiding principle. There are spiritual people involved, but also physical people. And circumcision, around which so much controversy has orbited (to this day), which became the sign of the covenant given in Genesis 17, can be viewed as a work or as a sign of grace. It all depends on whether a person is going to trust in the work and the sign itself, or in the grace of God which precedes it and looks forward to the future—grace that the recipient is not owed by God and is not automatically bestowed because of some birthright. Will they look to the types (circumcision, physical nation, plot of land in the Middle East) or to the antitypes[77] (circumcision of the heart, kingdom that cannot be seen, the new earth)? This is possible because, while gracious, Abraham's covenant(s) was never the Covenant of Grace.

---

[77] An antitype is not something opposed to a type (taking "anti" as meaning "against"). Rather, it is something that "corresponds to" (see 1 Pet 3:21 ESV) the type. It is the greater reality to which the type points.

Gracious Legal Covenants: Mosaic Covenant

(*The Prophetic Covenant*)

THE NEXT THREE COVENANTS we will inspect are bound together by the idea of "office." This is rarely noticed, and I will demonstrate the reason shortly. The Bible teaches us that Christ fulfilled three offices in his coming: The office of *prophet*, the office of *priest*, and the office of *king*. These offices were originally given to Adam to fulfill, but Adam failed. After Adam, the duties of these three offices were often merged together such that a person like Abraham could be viewed in some sense as a prophet (Gen 20:7), in some sense as a king (Gen 17:6), and in some sense as a priest (Gen 22:2).

The offices eventually became distinct, but three unique typological covenants were given to help us identify the function and importance of each office for fulfilling the Covenant of Works. Yet, the heads of these covenants never carried out their duties to perfection, and thus none of them were ever considered to be The Prophet, The Priest, or The King. Those were left to prophecy. Because of this, Messianic expectations arose in the community which in some way anticipated the climax of these in a single person. Each of these OT covenants anticipated, and each office bearer heralded, the coming of the man who would bear all three offices in his person, carrying their duties out to perfection.

Moses the Prophet

The first covenant we will look at is the Mosaic covenant or what I refer to as the Prophetic Covenant. God used Moses to be his great prophet to the people. "There has not arisen a prophet since in Israel like Moses, whom the LORD knew face to face" (Deut 34:10). While most people think of prophets as *fore*tellers (they know the future), the reality is that most of their time was spent *forth*telling (speaking truth).

Moses and the Law

Moses spoke the truth of God through a covenant. Later prophets would speak the truth of God by bringing covenant lawsuits against the people. When they broke God's law, the covenant sanctions would be brought down upon through the prophetic warnings until they repented. Many prophetic books can be viewed as covenantal lawsuits, which bring the charges, expect repentance, and foreshadow and predict the coming great covenant keeper—the Messiah.

God made a covenant with Israel through Moses. "The LORD said to Moses, 'Write these words, for in accordance with these words I have made a covenant with you and with Israel'" (Ex 34:27). What were these words specifically? It says, "He wrote on the tablets the words of the covenant, <u>the Ten Commandments</u>" (Ex 34:28) and "He declared to you his covenant, which he commanded you to perform, that is, <u>the Ten Commandments</u>, and he wrote them on two tablets of stone" (Deut 4:13). These "words" were then kept in the "ark of the covenant" (Deut 10:2). Clearly then, law is part and parcel of the Mosaic covenant.

The Law and This Covenant

At this point, because the Mosaic covenant is one of the most misunderstood of all biblical covenants, we want to make a few important observations. First, it is not everything in the Law (i.e. *Torah*) which is, properly speaking, the Mosaic covenant. Rather, it is the Ten Commandments and those aspects of the Law which elaborate them. These elaborations may be thought of as Israel's "case law." The Reformed call them judicial law or civil law. Case law is the specific application of a moral law or principle to a given situation in the national life of a people. In the instance of Israel, this was temporary case law commanded by God through Moses to give to that people to order its civil affairs.

For example, a man dies with leaving only daughters, but there are no provisions for passing on his land to daughters; what should we do about this? A boy picks up sticks on the Sabbath day; what should we do with him?[78] Moses is too burdened to judge all the people, how do we settle this problem? It is probably the case that all case law relates to the Ten Commandments. Yet, there are still other (ceremonial) laws in the Pentateuch, but these are not properly speaking part of the Mosaic covenant. We discuss these in the next chapter.[79]

---

[78] Because Israel is a theocracy, its civil and ceremonial life was not segregated the way ours is, except in the form of specific priestly duties that were to be carried out by a special priestly tribe. We will discuss this in the next chapter. For now, just note how *sabbath* has the idea of both rest and worship. Yet, this kind of law is properly speaking a civil law, because it deals with ordinary life.

[79] Together with moral and civil, the ceremonial law creates the famous three-fold division of the law (Westminster Confession of Faith 19.3-4; 1689 London Baptist Confession 19.3-4) that goes back at least as far as Aquinas (1225-1274) who wrote, "The ceremonial precepts relate to God, so do the judicial precepts relate to one's neighbor" (*Summa*, I-II q.104 a.1 obj.3) and even farther back to Augustine, Tertullian, and Justin Martyr. See Jonathan F. Bayes, *The Threefold Division of the Law* (The Christian Institute,

Second, the Ten Commandments are themselves a republication of the eternal moral standards that God built into the very fabric of creation and published more generally on the human heart in the Covenant of Works. There are a couple of things to flesh out here. First, notice I said a republication of the *eternal moral standards*, not a republication of the Covenant of Works. Second, the Mosaic Covenant is not, properly speaking, the Covenant of Works, though as we said in the Introduction to these OT covenants, it could be and often was approached as if it were.

Third, recognize that it isn't like no one knew that it was wrong to murder prior to Mt. Sinai or that God did not hold men accountable to it. Some Christians give the impression by their view of "we are not under law but under grace," that it is almost as if God came down to Moses and created these Ten Commandments out of thin air just for these Israelites and no one else. But Cain murdered his brother (Gen 4:8) long before God told Moses, "You shall not murder" (Ex 20:13), and God held him accountable for that action (Gen 4:10-12). Indeed, we find violations and awareness of *every one* of the Ten Commandments prior to Mt. Sinai.[80] Of course, even pagan law codes such as Hamurabbi knew of them.

Fourth, everyone knows what they are supposed to do, at least generally speaking, in terms of the Ten Command-

---

2005). http://www.christian.org.uk/html-publications/theology/threefold.pdf, last accessed 10-14-2014.

[80] First: Josh 24:2; Second: Gen 31:32; Third: Gen 4:26 (taking *chalal* as "pollute" rather than "calling upon" the name); Fourth: Gen 2:2-3, 7:2, 8:10, 12, 29:18, Ex 12:15; Fifth: Gen 9:22, 49:4; Sixth: Gen 4:8, 34:25; Seventh: Gen 49:4; Eighth: Gen 31:32, 44:8; Ninth: Gen 4:9; Tenth: Gen 3:6.

ments—because all people are born with the law written on their heart (Rom 2:15). This law was embedded into creation in the Covenant of Creation as I have shown. I believe it proves that everyone on earth is held accountable to the Covenant of Works quite apart from having received an OT covenant. To put it another way, Israelites did not need to be put under the Covenant of Works. They were already born into it. The Apostle seems to make this very point (without using "covenant") when he says that from Adam to Moses, everyone died (Rom 5:12-14). Death is the result of the breaking of the pre-Fall covenant in the Garden of Eden.

This kind of knowledge explains things like the pagan Hamurabbi law code (see above). It would include knowing that they should not worship other gods, created lesser beings than Yahweh who deceived the people (Ps 82:1-5), or physical created beings like birds and animals, or even gods of their own imagination or pleasure (such as their stomach; Php 3:19). Yet, they worshiped and served the creation rather than the Creator, and they knew it was wrong, and they are held accountable for it (Rom 1:25ff). It would include even the idea of Sabbath (which means "rest"), for all people know inherently that they need to rest and that this rest needs to be set aside for some kind of spiritual-religious purpose. This is why even secular people in Colorado go up to the mountains on a weekend and call it a "spiritual experience." How do they know these things? It is because this is a reflection of the covenantal ordinances that are written upon their hearts. In as much as this Prophetic Covenant is about law, it offers no reprieve, no consolation, and no comfort for failure. It is a reminder of what we have all done in Adam. Yet, blessings are held out for obedience and curses for disobedience. In this way, it is a reflection of the Covenant of Works, though not the Covenant of Works itself.

This leads to a final observation. The Ten Commandments—and especially their peculiar outworking in Israel's case law—were given for that specific people with very specific promises for them and them alone. This is the point of the lengthy sections of blessings and curses given to the nation of Israel in the Law (Lev 26; Deut 27-28). These were not promised to everyone, but to Israel alone. This does not mean that the Ten Commandments do not apply to anyone else in history, nor that God does not hold all people responsible for them, as we have seen. It is simply to say that the peculiar Mosaic economy was attached with specific promises that were not given to any other nation in that specific way. Still, generally speaking, it seems true that if a nation outwardly keeps the moral law, it will reap the blessings that come from having a just and moral society. If it breaks that law, they will eventually face the consequences. Israel's prophets make the later abundantly clear. But that is very different from claiming that God becomes the God of any nation in a special way, much less that they have a right to invoke specific covenantal blessings of the Jewish people.

Israel and the Law

All of these points are tied up in Israel's position as Yahweh's covenant nation, the corporate people who were to express his laws as a light to the world. Even though they were elect from among all the nations, they held the blessings of this position *conditionally*.[81] If they would obey, the nations would stream to them. But if they would not obey, the world would remain in darkness, and Israel itself would be punished.

However, because they were elected (Deut 7:6), because the promise of the Seed came through them, God had predetermined that one particular Israelite would fulfill the conditions of the covenant perfectly. He would be the Great Prophet. But in order for this Prophet to actually arrive before God wiped all his people off the face of their earth for their sins, it was necessary for this Prophetic Covenant to rest upon the earlier covenant that God made with Abraham (which as we have seen rests itself upon the even prior covenant given to Noah and Adam). This allows God to be gracious to Israel in the midst of the Prophetic Covenant that continually judges law-breakers.

Moses and God's Grace

Thus, there is grace in this covenant. It is grace that precedes and then attaches itself to the Mosaic covenant. We read that God brought Israel out of Egypt and made a covenant with them because "God heard their groaning, and God remembered his covenant with Abraham, with Isaac, and with Jacob" (Ex 2:24). The law that he gave them was preambled by this earlier covenant in such a way that it became part of the Ten Commandments: "And God spoke all these words, saying, 'I am the LORD your God, <u>who</u>

---

[81] This does not mean that all forms of election are conditional; they are not. It simply means that Israel is a type of a greater election to a greater kingdom.

brought you out of the land of Egypt, out of the house of
slavery. You shall have no other gods before me'" (Ex 20:1-
3). When they would break the covenant with Moses—the
Law—God would "for their sake remember the covenant
with their forefathers, whom I brought out of the land of
Egypt in the sight of the nations, that I might be their God: I
am the LORD" (Lev 26:45). Their forgiveness would be
based on the earlier promise.

Final Observations

Thus, as with the other OT covenants, there is an overlap of ideas: works and grace. The Mosaic covenant can be
viewed legally as of works, and simultaneously it can be
viewed graciously and of promise. This is because it is typological of the Covenant of Grace and a peculiar application of
the Covenant of Works in the life of a specific people. This
shows: 1. The need for the Covenant of Works to be fulfilled, 2. God's showing grace when the Covenant of Works
had not yet been fulfilled, and 3. God anticipating the time
when the Covenant of Works would be fulfilled in Christ.
This makes for a strange situation, one that we have a difficult time from our side of the cross relating to. It has given
rise to an almost endless debate over whether the Mosaic
covenant was gracious or rooted in works. The answer is,
without confusing the two, without merging them or blend-
ing them together, both elements are present. But this is what
I have already shown with the other OT covenants after the
Fall. In that respect, Moses isn't that much different from
Noah, except that there is a lot more law explicitly present.

Apart from the next covenant I will discuss, *as a nation* Israel was under the obligation of covenant law to keep it perfectly (Lev 19:2). If they did, they would live long in the land (Deut 4:40). But imperfect law keeping is not tolerated forever, as the people eventually learned, for it causes our hearts to grow cold towards God. As a Father, God disciplines his children so that they might return to him.

As individuals within that nation, the promise was always held out that they would live (apparently forever; Lev 18:5) … if they live perfectly (Lev 19:2; cf. Matt 5:48). But if they chose God's means of grace, if they would believe like Abraham did, they would be saved by grace. "The Lord said to Moses, Lo! I come to thee in a pillar of a cloud, that the people may hear me speaking to thee, and may believe (*pisteuō*) thee for ever: and Moses reported the words of the people to the Lord" (Ex 19:9 LXX). Instead we learn that most did not. "And when the LORD sent you from Kadesh-barnea, saying, 'Go up and take possession of the land that I have given you,' then you rebelled against the commandment of the LORD your God and did not believe him or obey his voice" (Deut 9:23). Thus, "I will turn away my face from them, and will show what shall happen to them in the last days; for it is a perverse generation, sons in whom is no faith" (Deut 32:20 LXX).

God established this Prophetic Covenant until the promised Prophet-Seed should come. This is as it was predicted. "The LORD your God will raise up for you a prophet like me from among you, from your brothers—it is to him you shall listen" (Deut 18:15). There had not arisen a prophet in Israel like Moses (Deut 34:10), until the Lord Jesus Christ came and fulfilled the promise (Acts 3:22; 7:37).

Gracious Legal Covenants:
Levitical Covenant

(*The Priestly Covenant*)

THE NEXT COVENANT IS WHAT I CALL the Priestly Covenant. This covenant is contained, literarily speaking (that is, in the literature of Moses), *within* the same texts as the Mosaic covenant. For this reason, it has rarely been discussed as a separate covenant worthy of its own place in a systematic treatment such as this one, though it sometimes has (often without understanding its implications).[82] But when systems fail to distinguish this covenant, they are doing so at the express rejection of the Scripture itself. Furthermore, it creates *much* unnecessary confusion.

Nehemiah refers to "the covenant of the <u>priesthood</u> and the <u>Levites</u>" (Neh 13:29). Malachi tells these priests, "You have corrupted the <u>covenant of Levi</u>" (Mal 2:8). Jeremiah likens this "covenant with the <u>Levitical priests</u>" to the "covenant with the day and night" (Jer 33:20) and the "covenant with David" (Jer 33:21), thereby placing it side by side as a standalone covenant of equal worth and importance.

This is not the covenant given to Moses, the covenant symbolized in the Ark of the Covenant. It is the covenant that figuratively and literally surrounds the Mosaic covenant like the Tabernacle and Temple surround the Ark. It is given

---

[82] For example, Roger T. Beckwith, "The Unity and Diversity of God's Covenants," *TynBul* 38:1 (1987): 92-118; Thomas Boston, *The Whole Works of the Late Reverend and Learned Mr. Thomas Boston*, 12 vols. (Aberdeen: George and Robert King, 1848).

for the protection of and the forgiveness for breaking the Prophetic Covenant. (Of course, it too could be broken). Since most are unfamiliar with this covenant, I should begin this examination by looking at why it is called the covenant of Levi.

Levi

Levi was the third oldest son of Jacob and Leah (Gen 29:34). He and his older brother Simeon got into big trouble from their father after they put to the sword an entire village for raping their sister Dinah (Gen 34:2, 25). For this, their father curses them saying, "I will scatter them in Jacob and disperse them in Israel" (Gen 49:7). Simeon is later absorbed into Judah (Josh 19:9) and is not mentioned in the tribal blessings of Deuteronomy 33. But God turns the curse for Levi into an unexpected blessing.

Malachi says that this covenant with Levi was one of "life and peace." It came because he "feared me. He stood in awe of my name … He walked with me in peace and uprightness, and turned many from iniquity" (Mal 2:5-8). After Malachi, the last book of our OT, was written, the Jews began to turn Levi's action at Shechem into a kind of zealous obedience for the law,[83] and it is possible to see this in some typological sense, especially when it is viewed in light of a story that comes much later through one of Levi's descendants, a grandson of Aaron, the man named Phinehas. Yet we must remember, Jacob cursed Levi because of what he did.

---

[83] Especially the book of Jubilees. See Jub 30:18; 31:11-17; 32:1-9. He is also singled out in Aramaic Levi, The Testament of Twelve Patriarchs, Joseph and Asenath, Ascension of Moses, and many others.

Phinehas

Numbers 25 tells about a horrific sight that begins to unfold at the entrance to the Tent of Meeting. It occurs after the men of Israel begin having relations with Moabite women who then entice them into sacrificing to, eating the covenant meals of, and bowing down to foreign gods. In this way, Israel began worshipping Baal of Peor. The LORD takes great offence at this, and commands that the chiefs of Israel be killed on the spot. Phinehas takes his spear and begins obeying the command of the LORD. For this, God rewards Phinehas with a great covenant promise, "Tell him I am making my covenant of peace with him. He and his descendants will have a covenant of a lasting priesthood" (Num 25:12-13). The Psalms have a short commentary on this passage. "But Phinehas stood up and intervened, and the plague was checked. This was credited to him as righteousness for endless generations to come" (Ps 106:30-31). Levi and Phinehas therefore have very similar stories. Since it is called the "covenant with Levi" rather than the "covenant with Phinehas," we know the Jews saw the roots of this covenant many centuries earlier than even Moses, in the life of Levi himself.

This is of no small importance. For if this covenant promise was given prior to Moses' birth, even if only in a shadowy way, then the covenant of Levi cannot be equated with the covenant of Moses any more than the Abrahamic covenant can. Indeed, we find that God actually chooses Aaron *because* he is a Levite (Ex 4:14; Num 3:16). Yes, Moses is also a Levite, and his sons get to participate in the Levitical covenant as other Levites do, but not as priests.[84] For a time, Moses even participates in the sprinkling of blood (Ex 24:6-9), and intercedes for the people like a priest (cf. Ex 32:30ff) and king[85] would do. But for the long-term, this role is reserved for the direct lineage of Aaron. The priestly duties of the Covenant of Levi are therefore passed down biologically, whereas the prophetic duties of the Covenant of Moses are passed through the prophets of Israel who were specially called by God as Moses was (Ex 3:1ff).

Aaron

At any rate, God gives Aaron a promise in line with Jacob's curse of Levi saying that he will have no inheritance (Num 18:20; cf. Gen 49:7), *but* he does so in the same manner that he spoke to Abraham when he gave Abraham his covenant saying, "I am your ..." (Num 18:20; cf. Gen 15:1, 18). What I am suggesting is that "I am your" is covenantal language. When God says these words, he is making a claim upon that person via a covenant, just as he did with Abraham. Thus, God sets the Levites apart for himself, unique among all other Israelites (Num 3:12; 8:18), and so the covenant of the priesthood is established.

---

[84] This is also a vital point. Aaron's sons are not prophets; Moses' are not priests. When the sons of Moses acted as priests in the territory of Dan (Jdg 18:30), Judges views this negatively, as a sign that everyone was doing what was right in his own eyes. This is like Korah, Moses' cousin and also a Levite, who wanted to be part of the Aaronic priesthood, because the menial tasks of the tabernacle were not good enough for him. In other words, Aaron and Moses, while Levites, demonstrate separate covenants.

[85] David intercedes for the people; 2 Sam 24:14; Ps 60:1, etc.

Priestly Covenantal Duty

It was the covenantal duty of the priests to serve and to guard the sanctuary and the covenant with Israel (cf. Num 3:18).[86] Thus, "Moses wrote this law and gave it to the priests, the sons of Levi, who carried the ark of the covenant of the LORD" (Deut 31:9). Theirs was a covenant within a covenant or perhaps a covenant after a covenant, much like the kingly covenant with David will be. God made a covenant with the Levites whereby they would help Israel keep the Mosaic Law, so that when they disobeyed, this covenant provided the means of forgiveness. The Levitical covenant was both legal in terms of its strict duties, but gracious in that it offered a way for those who broke the Prophetic Covenant to be forgiven in anticipation of the new covenant in Christ.

Priests would do this through specific duties pertaining to sacrifices (and the various duties of keeping the tabernacle/temple in order was part of this sacrificial system of duties). Like the sacrifices offered by Abel, Cain, Noah and others, they foreshadowed the person and work of Christ. Yet, they were legally obligated to keep them, because Christ had not yet come. They would do this in terms of the historically-specific national entity of Israel that was set apart from all the other nations as holy. The holiness codes, separation codes, purity codes, and cleanliness codes were a kind of case law for the Levitical covenant, having little specifically to do with the Ten Commandments, but everything to do with the purity of God's OT temple and people who walked within its midst.

---

[86] Here, the words *shamar* and *abad* are used, the same words/duty given to Adam in the Garden—Gen 2:15.

Deuteronomy vs. Leviticus

Generally speaking, you can observe and read about these two covenants in two different books. Deuteronomy (*Deutero*-"second," *nomos*-"law") is the covenant God gave to Moses and it is rooted in the republication of the Ten Commandments (Deut 5:1-33). Most, though not all, of Deuteronomy is spent discussing these commands, their case law, and the obligations Israel has to keep this covenant. It isn't really about the Levites at all.

But there is a different book in the Torah that has very different material in it, material that looks little like the Ten Commandments or its case law, though it does have a small amount of that in it. The title of this book ought to give away its importance to this Priestly Covenant. It is called *Leviticus* and it deals mostly with the regulations given specifically to the priests of Israel and the Levites. Think about it. A whole book of the Bible dedicated to a covenant that few even know exists. Yet, chapter after chapter delineates the tedious and sometimes strange duties of the priests. Other Israelites were not obligated to keep this covenant, except vicariously through the priest. But it was the priests and Levites who had all of the actual ministries to obey. When others presumed that they should be allowed to act as intercessory priests, God put them to death.[87] God set this covenant in place until the promised priestly Seed would come.

---

[87] See the rebellion of Korah (a Levite but not from Aaron's specific line) and his friend Dathan (from the tribe of Reuben; Num 16). See also n. 83.

Gracious Legal Covenants: Davidic Covenant

(*The Kingly Covenant*)

THE FINAL OT COVENANT we will look at is the Davidic covenant. I call this the Kingly Covenant. Israel had asked Samuel to give them a king (1 Sam 8:5). Many people think that this was in and of itself a sin, since God tells them, "They have rejected me from being king over them" (1 Sam 8:7). However, Deuteronomy does not say it was wrong to ask for a king. "When you come to the land that the LORD your God is giving you, and you possess it and dwell in it and then say, 'I will set a king over me, like all the nations that are around me,' you may indeed set a king over you" (Deut 17:14). There were, however, stipulations. He had to be the one "whom the LORD your God will choose." He had to be "from among your brothers." He could not be a foreigner (Deut 17:15).

Saul

When Israel asked for a king, they wanted him to be a king like all the other nations (1 Sam 8:5). This was the problem; this was a rejection of Yahweh. For them this meant this king would be exceedingly tall and handsome, and they didn't care where he came from. So God gave them Saul (1 Sam 9:2). While it tells us that this was the man whom God chose (1 Sam 10:1), it also tells us that his choice was to give them the man whom *they* chose (1 Sam 12:13). This was not God's first choice, as is made clear when God does choose his king: the man David (2 Sam 6:21; 1 Kgs 11:32).

David

David was not like Saul. He was average rather than extraordinary. He was the runt of his father Jesse's litter. But he was a man after God's own heart (1 Sam 13:14) and importantly, he came from the line that God had chosen long ago to be the seed through which Messiah would come. Unlike Saul—the Benjamite (1 Sam 9:21), David was from the line of Judah (Ruth 4:17-22). God had told Judah through his father Jacob, "Judah is a lion's cub; from the prey, my son, you have gone up. He stooped down; he crouched as a lion and as a lioness; who dares rouse him? The scepter shall not depart from Judah, nor the ruler's staff from between his feet, until tribute comes to him; and to him shall be the obedience of the peoples" (Gen 49:9-10).

Once Samuel had anointed David (1 Sam 16:8-13), God entered into a covenant with him. As it says, "I have made a covenant with my chosen one; I have sworn to David my servant" (Ps 89:3). This covenant is recorded in 2 Samuel with the familiar "seed" language, "When your days are fulfilled and you rest with your fathers, I will set up your seed after you, who will come from your body, and I will establish his kingdom. He shall build a house for My name, and I will establish the throne of his kingdom forever" (2 Sam 7:12-13 NKJV).

Solomon

As with many prophecies, this one has a near and far fulfillment. The near fulfillment was Solomon. Solomon was David and Bathsheba's second son (the first one died), and it was he who would rule the kingdom as king. From Solomon would come a whole line of kings that would rule the southern half of the divided kingdom known as Judah. They were to rule over Israel, upholding God's law in the land or else punishment would come and Israel would be given over to a foreign nation. The Kingly Covenant was not the right of every Israelite as the Mosaic covenant was (distinguishing between those who must keep the covenant vs. those who prophetically speak out as covenant ambassadors). Rather, it was like the Priestly Covenant, given to them for this specific purpose until the promised kingly Seed would come.

Like the Priestly Covenant, this Kingly Covenant was more like a covenant grant than it was a suzerain treaty. God swore to David that his sons would sit on the throne forever. And yet, there are aspects of this covenant that are quite conditional. "If your sons keep my covenant and my testimonies that I shall teach them, their sons also forever shall sit on your throne" (Ps 132:12). Narrowly speaking, the laws of this covenant would be things like not acquiring too many horses or wives, and most of all living according to a copy of the Ten Commandments as approved by the Levitical priests that he was to keep by his throne. These terms are set out in Deuteronomy (Deut 17:15-20). Thus, like the Levites, the king was to be a guardian of the Mosaic covenant. The kings and the priests guard the law. His behavior and laws were to be governed by God's, showing himself loyal to the Great Suzerain who had given him this gracious covenant grant. David and Solomon's era were considered the golden age in the history of God's people, until the greater King would come and usher in the everlasting kingdom.

Concluding Thoughts

A word should be made about how God dealt with Israel in terms of these three covenantal offices. Individual responsibility was critical for how God dealt with a person (as faith was always a necessary part of the covenantal relationship). But the nation was judged by how its prophets, priests, and kings behaved in relation to their covenantal obligations. "In the prophets of Jerusalem I have seen a horrible thing: they commit adultery and walk in lies; they strengthen the hands of evildoers, so that no one turns from his evil; all of them have become like Sodom to me, and its inhabitants like Gomorrah" (Jer 23:14). "The prophets prophesy falsely, and the priests rule at their direction; my people love to have it so, but what will you do when the end comes?" (Jer 5:31). "As a thief is shamed when caught, so the house of Israel shall be shamed: they, their kings, their officials, their priests, and their prophets" (Jer 2:26). "In that day, declares the LORD, courage shall fail both king and officials. The priests shall be appalled and the prophets astounded" (Jer 4:9). "Behold, I will fill with drunkenness all the inhabitants of this land: the kings who sit on David's throne, the priests, the prophets, and all the inhabitants of Jerusalem" (Jer 13:13). This shows the importance of these three covenants and the *representatives* God gave to Israel to oversee them. Representation is a key element in all of these covenants.

The Covenant of Grace

(*The New Covenant; The Sabbath Covenant*)

New Covenant Predicted

WE COME NOW TO THE CULMINATION, the redemptive-historical climax, the final covenant. It is predicted in the OT in what Jeremiah refers to as "the new covenant."

> Behold, the days are coming, declares the LORD, when I will make a <u>new covenant</u> with the house of Israel and the house of Judah, not like the covenant that I made with their fathers on the day when I took them by the hand to bring them out of the land of Egypt, my covenant that they broke, though I was their husband, declares the LORD. For this is the covenant that I will make with the house of Israel after those days, declares the LORD: I will put my law within them, and I will write it on their hearts. And I will be their God, and they shall be my people. And no longer shall each one teach his neighbor and each his brother, saying, 'Know the LORD,' for they shall all know me, from the least of them to the greatest, declares the LORD. For I will forgive their iniquity, and I will remember their sin no more (Jer 31:31-34).

Exegesis: Jeremiah's New Covenant Prophecy

First, an exegesis of this passage is in order. Jeremiah speaks of coming days, which in biblical parlance refers to the last days. In the "last days" God speaks to us by "his son" (Heb 1:2). In other words, there is some sense in which the last days are here in our own day—today. There is also, of course, a sense in which the Last Day is not yet here, and we must keep these two ideas in tension as the NT does. Keeping with our analogy of a "week" using Paul's words, the seventh day is giving way to the eschatological eighth day of the new heavens and earth. (We will discuss the importance of this eighth day later on; see Rom 13:12). It is because the last days are here today that the NT repeatedly quotes this passage saying that this new covenant has been inaugurated in Christ (Luke 22:20; 1 Cor 11:25; 2 Cor 3:6; Heb 8:8, 13; 9:15; 12:24). In other words, whatever Jeremiah is talking about, it is in at least some sense here now, which is why (as we will see), this passage is quoted in the NT.

Houses of Israel and Judah

Jeremiah says that the LORD will make this new covenant with the "house of Israel and the house of Judah." Since the NT says that the new covenant is made with those who drink Christ's blood (speaking not literally, but sacramentally of the Lord's Supper),[88] we have to understand that making a new covenant with the house of Israel refers eschatologically to the church, which is called by various OT titles including *ekklesia* (church),[89] the circumcision,[90] a kingdom of priests (which is important for baptism),[91] and as it regards Jeremi-

---

[88] To Jews in Luke 22:20; to Gentiles in 1 Cor 11:25.
[89] Obviously "church" is a NT term, but it is deeply rooted in the LXX (Greek) OT for the very special assembly of Yahweh around the covenant: Deut 4:10; 9:10; 18:16; 23:2-4; 31:30, etc.
[90] Php 3:3. Circumcision is also rooted in OT covenant.
[91] Compared Ex 19:6 with Rev 1:6 and 5:10.

ah's prophecy—true Jews,[92] and the Israel of God.[93] If God is not making this new covenant with the church, then it would make no sense for the NT to apply it to the church, even though Jeremiah also happened to apply it in some more immediate context to the nation of Israel.

Not Like the Previous Covenant

It says that this new covenant will not be "like the covenant that I made with their fathers on the day when I took them by the hand to bring them out of the land of Egypt, my covenant that they broke." This seems to refer especially to the Prophetic Covenant given by God to the people through the prophet Moses, as Jeremiah then talks about the law written on the heart, but priestly and kingly case laws are not written on anyone's heart. So the Apostle explains, "This is what I mean: the law, which came 430 years afterward, does not annul a covenant previously ratified by God, so as to make the promise void" (Gal 3:17). Jeremiah is teaching that the new covenant will not be like the Prophetic Covenant, not that somehow the moral law no longer exists, but that our obedience to this covenant will no longer be the judiciary means of cursing or blessing for covenant-community promises. Rather, someone else will keep this covenant perfectly on our behalf, and it is through faith in his covenant keeping that blessings follow.[94] This is the whole point of Hebrews'

---

[92] Rom 2:28-29. The word "Jew" comes from Judah and it means "praise." Paul makes a word play on Judah in this passage.

[93] Gal 6:16. "Israel" is Jacob's covenantal name.

[94] Curses will also follow from the rejection of Christ. This is what makes it worse to reject Christ than to die in your sins (under the covenant of works) having never heard about Christ. This is a double curse.

argument that the new covenant has come and that Christ is its representative head (more on this below).

My Law in their Heart

Jeremiah then explains what this covenant will include. "I will put my law within them, and I will write it on their hearts. And I will be their God, and they shall be my people." If you recall our short discussion under the "Covenant of Redemption" on the subjective and objective nature of redemption, this is the subjective part. In this new covenant, God will save a peculiar people. The law will be written on their hearts.

But someone will raise the objection that even in the old covenant, some people had the law written on their hearts. Doesn't Paul say that even Gentiles had the law written on their hearts? (Rom 2:14-15). No, that isn't *exactly* what he says. He says that they have the "works of the law", or as one translation puts it, the "requirements" of the law written on their hearts. That is, the law accuses them and defends them through their consciences. What law? The moral law. But the tablet remains the same as it was for Israel: stone. Their hearts are stone. Thus Martin Luther concludes, "The knowledge of the work is written, that is, the law that is written in letters concerning the works that have to be done, but not the grace to fulfill this law."[95]

But someone might say, "What about the saved Israelites? An example might be King Josiah when it says that there was no king like him, 'who turned to the LORD with all his

---

[95] Martin Luther, *Commentary on* Romans (2:14).

heart and with all his soul and with all his might, according to all the Law of Moses (2 Kgs 23:35). Also, the Psalmist says that the law of God is in his heart (Ps 37:31; 40:8). Don't they have the law written on their heart?" This isn't technically the same thing as what Jeremiah is talking about either. No one doubts that OT saints were saved by God. When they were saved, they had new desires to actually want to keep the law of God. But Jeremiah has something more specific in mind.

The idea of the law written on your heart refers to *the place* where the law is kept. For the prophet, this is connected to the repository for the Ten Commandments: The temple. Remember, the Ark of the Covenant held the Commandments, and this was put into the Most Holy Place inside the temple. In the OT, God resided in the midst of the people in this special holy residence. The Commandments were put in there, and the people had to make copies of them and teach them to their children (Deut 7:7-9). They were saved by faith, looking to the forgiveness that was made available to them in the temple sacrifices which prefigured the once-for-all sacrifice of the Messiah.

In the NT, however, the temple is transformed (which, as we will see, is another link between OT Israel and the NT church). First, Jesus becomes the very temple of God (John 1:14;[96] 2:19-21). Second, when he goes away he sends the Spirit and the Christian becomes a temple (1 Cor 6:19), as does the entire church which is now made of "living stones" (2 Cor 3:3; 1 Pet 2:4-5). Thus, God no longer resides in a temple made by hands in one stationary location, but in his

---

[96] Literally, Jesus "tabernacles" among us in the flesh.

church and in his movable saints scattered throughout the world. This refers to the Holy Spirit as is understood in a parallel passage in Ezekiel, "I will give you a new heart, and a new spirit I will put within you. And I will remove the heart of stone from your flesh and give you a heart of flesh. And I will put my Spirit within you, and cause you to walk in my statutes and be careful to obey my rules" (Ezek 36:26-27).

No Longer Teach his Brother and the Incarnation of Christ

This is significant for understanding the last part of Jeremiah's prophecy, "No longer shall each one teach his neighbor and each his brother, saying, 'Know the LORD,' for they shall all know me, from the least of them to the greatest, declares the LORD." Though this can be understood in subjective terms (personal salvation), there is also (perhaps mostly) something objective going on here. "Knowing the LORD" does not refer to the eradication of evangelism, preaching, teaching, and discipleship in the new covenant, because somehow everyone magically knows everything at the moment of conversion. It refers to the coming of Jesus in the flesh. This is made intelligible by the story of Samuel.

It says that "Samuel did not yet <u>know the Lord</u>, and <u>the Word of the Lord</u> had not yet been revealed" (1 Sam 3:7). What this means is nothing short of astonishing. The context is more than Samuel hearing a voice calling his name ("Samuel, Samuel"). It begins by saying that "The <u>Word</u> of the Lord was rare in those days; there was no frequent <u>vision</u>" (1 Sam 3:1). One does not hear visions. One *sees* them. Samuel finally figures out what is going on when "the Lord came and stood" before him (1 Sam 3:10). Voices do not stand. People do.

This is an appearance of none other than the pre-incarnate Christ, also called the Angel of the LORD. In the OT, Christ came to people too, but it was a select, rare group that included Adam and Eve (Gen 3:8-4:1), Cain (Gen 4:6-15), Job (Job 38:1ff), Abraham (Gen 22:15; cf. 12:1-3; 15:1-21; 18:1-33; 22:1-18), Hagar (Gen 16:7), Jacob (Gen 32:24-28), Moses (Ex 3:2-6), Balaam (Num 22:22-35), Joshua (Josh 5:13-15), Gideon (Jdg 5:11-18), Samson's mother and father (Jdg 16:3-21), Samuel (1 Sam 3:1-21), Elijah (1 Kgs 19:7), Isaiah (Isa 6:1ff), Jeremiah (Jer 1:4-11), Daniel (Dan 7:13), Ezekiel (Ezek 1:28), Zechariah (Zech 3:1-6), and presumably the prophets of Israel who received the "word of the LORD." In fact, this Angel is the covenant LORD—the one who entered into covenant (Jdg 2:1ff) with Israel and took her as his possession (Deut 32:9; cf. 7-8). No ordinary angel could enter into a covenant with Israel and forgive their sins (Ex 23:20-21).

This becomes extremely important for the idea of continuity, for it is Christ who is making covenants in both testaments with Israel—one in the form of types, the other as antitypes. But the point here is, the rest of the people did not know the Lord via a sensory saturated self-disclosure. As the Gospel of John says, "He was in the world [that is, the world of the OT], and the world was made through him, yet the world did not know him" (John 1:10). They had to take these people at their word (and often they didn't and got into big trouble for it).

Based on Samuel, who did not know the Lord until he stood in front of him, we can say that Jeremiah (who was himself called by the Word in a vision; cf. Jer 1, esp. vs. 9) is predicting the incarnation of Christ in the flesh. To "know the Lord" would no longer be to believe by hearsay, but as 1 John says, "That which was from the beginning, which we have <u>heard</u>, which we have <u>seen</u> with our eyes, which we looked upon and have <u>touched</u> with our hands, concerning the <u>word</u> of life—the life was made <u>manifest</u>, and we have seen it, and testify to it and proclaim to you the eternal life" (1 John 1:1-2). For it is at this time that God revealed himself publically to all flesh by human flesh. Notice how both John and Samuel speak about the Word and thus knowing God.

There is, of course, a subjective part of this as well, for Jesus gave personal knowledge of himself to his elect so that the words of the prophecy, "I will forgive their iniquity, and I will remember their sin no more" becomes applicable to those who trust in Christ by faith. While everyone now knows the Lord objectively through Jesus who "has made him known" (John 1:18). "We know that we have come to know him, if we keep his commandments" (1 John 2:3).

New Covenant Inaugurated

The NT tells us that this new covenant is here today. It refers to its being put into effect by the death-blood of Christ (Heb 9:16-18). Thus, the Lord's Supper is "the new covenant in my blood" (Luke 22:20; 1 Cor 11:25). Jesus' new covenant speaks a better word than the old, even the covenant God made with Adam, Eve, and Abel, for his blood is better than theirs (Heb 12:24). So let us now look at how the new covenant is better than the old covenant.

"New" but not "Brand New"

First, let us understand the word "new" in "new covenant." This is an important word study, because many people want to say that the new covenant is "brand new." Of the eight occurrences of "new covenant" in Scripture, the word used seven of eight times for "new" (including the Greek of Jeremiah) is *kainos* (Jer 31:31 LXX; Luke 22:20; 1 Cor 11:25; 2 Cor 3:6; Heb 8:8, 13; 9:15). One time the word is *neos* (Heb 12:24). These words are *not* synonyms.[97] *Kainos* contemplates from the aspect of quality. *Neos* contemplates from the aspect of time. *Neos* seeks to create something brand new. *Kainos* seeks to improve something that is inferior, outworn, or marred through age.

So for example, Windows 8 (as of the writing of this book) is *kainos*. But the first Windows was *neos*. They are related, but only one was "brand new." When Coke came out with a "new" (and extremely unsuccessful) formula a couple decades ago, this was *kainos*. Diet Coke, Vanilla Coke, Coke Plus, Coca-Cola Zero, these are all *kainos*, improved or altered versions of Coke (notice, they are all still called "Coke"). But when Coke came out for the first time as a product, it was *neos*. *Kainos* is organically related to that which comes before it. So you have the "new Jerusalem" (Rev 3:12), or the "new name" (Rev 2:17), or a "new song" (Rev 14:3), or the "new heavens and earth" (Rev 21:1). These are not *neos*, but *kainos*.

---

[97] The classic study on this is Richard Chenevix Trench, *Synonyms of the New Testament*, 9th ed., improved. (Bellingham, WA: Logos Bible Software, 2003), 219-25.

Many people think of the new covenant as *neos*—brand spanking new like a baby out of the womb--and that is not wrong, so long as it is understood that this is in reference to the covenant head: Jesus is not Moses (or Adam, Noah, Abraham, Levi, or David for that matter). Though like us in one respect (he is fully human), he is quite unlike us in another (he is fully God). Notice the context of the only time *neos* is used for the new covenant, "Jesus, the <u>mediator</u> of a new (*neos*) covenant, and to the sprinkled blood that speaks a <u>better</u> word than the blood of Abel" (Heb 12:24). The context is Jesus as the mediator of this covenant. <u>He</u> is the *neos* of the new covenant.

But as it concerns, say, the relation of the new covenant to the law, this is not *neos*, as so many suppose. It is *kainos*. Jesus says, "A new [*kainos*] law I give to you that you love one another" (John 13:34). This makes sense, because it is not a brand spanking new commandment that we love one another. The OT is full of that language, as Jesus himself says, when he summarizes the OT in this very way (Matt 22:37-40; Mark 12:30-31; Luke 10:27; cf. Deut 6:5; Lev 19:18). Thus, John can say, "I am writing you no new commandment, but an old commandment that you had from the beginning. The old commandment is the word that you have heard. At the same time, it is a new commandment that I am writing to you, which is true in him and in you, because the darkness is passing away and the true light is already shining" (1 John 2:7-8). And again, "Not as though I were writing you a new commandment, but the one we have had from the beginning—that we love one another" (2 John 1:5).

"Better"

With this in mind, let us consider how the new covenant is "better" (a synonym for *kainos*). Hebrews is the main place that this language is used. It says that Jesus has a better name (Heb 1:4), a better priesthood (Heb 7:16; 22-24), offers a better sacrifice (Heb 9:23), is a better mediator (Heb 8:6), and therefore we have a better hope (Heb 7:19), built on better promises (Heb 8:6).

In these instances, it becomes important to maintain the difference between the priestly and prophetic covenants. It is not the moral, but the ceremonial that is better. These instances refer to Aaron's priesthood and intercession for the people, to the priests' job of offering sacrifices and going into the Tabernacle or Temple to do so. Even in the one place where it says that it is a *neos* covenant, it then says that Jesus' <u>blood</u> and <u>sacrifice</u> is "better" (Heb 12:24). Why? Because his "takes away" sin (Heb 10:4), it does not merely cover it. Again, this is priestly language. It is better because Jesus is unlike any that came before him. In that sense, he is truly *neos* in relation to all the old things.

Relationship: New Covenant to OT Gracious Covenants

I want to turn your attention now to the six various OT covenants (Adam, Noah, Abraham, the prophet, the priest, and the king). What is the relationship between the new covenant and these covenants? I want to view this relationship from the perspective of the suzerain treaty, the covenant grant, and the creation week analogy. I will look first at the suzerain treaty.

Suzerain Treaty

As we recall, the suzerain treaty has at its root the idea of works via stipulations or laws. Each of the old covenants has some kind of works principle, because the Covenant of Works stands behind the Covenant of Grace, just as justice stands behind pardon in a court of law. Each of these old covenants stand in contrast to the new covenant which finds its legal fulfillment in the meritorious works of Jesus Christ, the one "born under law" (Gal 4:4), who "fulfilled all righteousness" (Matt 3:15).

Thus, Adam is the "first man" and Christ is the last man (1 Cor 15:45). This "last Adam" title of Christ refers to the Adamic Works-Life-Creation covenant that Jesus is obeying, rather than to the gracious covenant made after the Fall with the same individual.

Similarly, the Levitical covenant with its ceremonial duty is a reflection of the same pre-Fall covenant and is thus called the "first covenant" (Heb 9:18-19), even though it is neither first in terms of time nor in terms of having a legal foundation. It was not the first expression of sacrifice in the context of covenant in the Scripture. Following this covenantal strand, Abel's sacrifice is contrasted to Christ and the new covenant (Heb 12:24). Noah sacrificed on the mountain when God made a covenant with him (Gen 8:21-9:16). Abraham was to offer Isaac his son as a sacrifice (Gen 22:2). And so on. Jesus' sacrifice is better than all those OT covenantal sacrifices.

The "old covenant" (2 Cor 3:14), which refers to Moses and the "reading of the law," in the only time the language is used, reflects the pre-Fall covenant. In fact, even though it is prior to the Mosaic or Levitical covenants, even Abraham's sign of circumcision ("the covenant of circumcision;" Acts 7:8) is equated with law-keeping (Acts 15; Rom 2:25-27; Gal 5:3), thus placing that covenant in some kind of opposition to the new covenant.[98]

The new covenant removes the obligation of our own perfect law keeping to merit life once-for-all. That is how it is the last covenant. No longer is our relation to God and covenant blessing: Do this and live (Lev 18:5; Gal 3:12). Yet, we are not freed from our relation to the law in every sense; we are freed from this particular relation that we have to it. This freedom ironically allows us to serve one another in love, thereby obeying the law (Gal 5:13-14). Our obedience is not our righteousness. Christ's obedience is—for those who trust in it by faith alone. "Christ is the end of the law for righteousness to everyone who believes" (Rom 10:4). "Not having a righteousness of my own that comes from the law, but that which comes through faith in Christ, the righteousness from God that depends on faith" (Php 3:9). There is indeed a newness here, but it is not what many suppose (i.e. that the law itself is new).

Each of these OT covenants had a covenant head. Adam was the head of his covenant, meaning that his obedience or

---

[98] People often get confused and think that Paul's "old" covenant is the same as Hebrew's "first" covenant. But a careful reading of these passages will demonstrate clearly that Paul has in mind the Ten Commandments (moral law), while Hebrews has in mind ceremonial priestly duty and isn't talking about moral law at all. The similar language ("first" and "old") only goes to show that in some sense, all of the old covenants were incomplete and could be viewed from the perspective of incomplete law-keeping. Hence, Abraham and his circumcision which is later reconfirmed in the Mosaic covenant (Acts 15:1, 5), or Noah and what was done in his tent which is likewise codified in law (Lev 18:7; 20:11; cf. Gen 9:22-23), etc.

disobedience brought covenant blessings or curses upon his posterity. Noah was the head of his covenant as were Abraham, Moses, Levi, and David. In the case of Abraham, God reaffirms his covenant with Isaac and Jacob. In the case of Levi, it is with Aaron and Phinehas and Zadok. With David it is with Solomon, Rehoboam, and all the kings of Judah. What each of these men have in common is … sin. They are all sinners. Thus, each failed to maintain the legal obligations of their covenant under that large umbrella called the Old Testament (or "covenant"). Adam ate the fruit. Noah drank it. Abraham laughed at God and tried to bring about the promise his way. Moses struck the rock. Levi put an entire city to death under false pretenses. David murdered his friend after sleeping with his wife.

But when Jesus comes along, he becomes the "Greater _____." Jesus is the Last Adam (1 Cor 15:45); the Greater Noah (1 Pet 3:20-21); the Greater Abraham (John 8:58); The Greatest Prophet (Acts 3:22-23); the Highest High Priest (to whom Levi paid a tithe; Heb 7:7-9); and David's Greater Son (Matt 22:45). It is just here that we discover the reason for these being called "covenants of promise" (Eph 2:12; Heb 8:6). For in whatever capacity these men stood and fell as covenant heads, Jesus stands firm and tall. Sin comes in through Adam, the gift comes through Christ (Rom 5:12-21). Death through flood came to the world through Noah, resurrection through the waters comes through Christ (1 Pet 3:20-22). And so on.

Thus, the new covenant is legal in at least two senses. First, Christ obeyed the law perfectly so that God can credit his righteousness to our account. In this way, the Covenant of Works is fulfilled perfectly in the new covenant—the second Adam. Second, our obedience to the law in the new covenant flows out of gratitude (as it was always supposed to), but in view of the now completed work of Christ on our behalf. Thus "we are released from the law, having died to that which held us captive, so that we serve in the new way of the Spirit and not in the old way of the written code" (Rom 7:6).

Covenant Grant: Fulfillment

We can look at the new covenant in terms of a covenant grant enacted in Christ's death. In fact, Hebrews refers to it as the effecting of a will (Heb 9:16-17), which is very much like a grant. This covenant grant is made possible because of Christ's fulfillment and obedience to the Covenant of Works and the legal principle that remained in each of the old covenants. But since each of the old covenants anticipated this, they can also be called covenants of promise (Eph 2:12). So what is the grant in the new covenant?

The grant is the antitypical fulfillment of the grants given in the OT. The most basic and important grant is Christ himself. God promised Eve a Seed (Gen 3:15), and Christ is the Seed fulfilled (Gal 3:16). He becomes ours by faith.

The other grants first and foremost belong to Christ, and then to us through union with him. God (re)granted <u>dominion</u> to Noah (Gen 9:2). Dominion is given to Christ (Dan 7:14; Eph 1:21). Through Christ we begin to carry it out into eternity (Matt 16:18; 1 Cor 6:3; Rev 4:4).

God granted to Abraham a <u>land</u> (Gen 15:7). In Christ (who is our Land and our Rest), the typological land becomes a kingdom (John 18:36). Jesus gives the Kingdom and its keys to us (Luke 6:20; Matt 16:19). This Kingdom is today invisible, but on the Last Day it will be the whole earth (Matt 5:5; Rom 4:13).

God granted to Abraham a nation (Gen 12:2). Christ inherits the nations (Ps 2:8; 82:8). Today Christians of all races belong to one another (Eph 4:4). We are a "holy nation" (1 Pet 2:9), made up of people from all nations (Isa 66:18; 19; Rev 5:9).

God granted to Moses and Aaron a tabernacle (Ex 25:9), and to David a temple (1 Sam 7:2-3). Christ is the holy tabernacle (John 1:14) and temple (John 2:21). We inherit the fullness of that holy sanctuary by becoming temples (1 Cor 6:19) in his NT temple, the church (Eph 2:20-22; 1 Pet 2:5).

To that end, the NT is clear that sacrifices that atone for sin, temples made of stone that mediate the presence of God, and other such typological things have passed away. Yet, there is even continuity in respects that most do not realize. We are not to offer animal sacrifices, *but our own bodies* as "living sacrifices" (Rom 12:1-2; Heb 13:16). Our prayers are the golden bowls of incense in the very temple of God (Rev 5:8). We have drink offerings of suffering (Php 2:17), fragrant offerings of giving money (Php 4:18), and offer the fragrant aroma of the gospel ministry (2 Cor 2:14-15), and the priestly duty of preaching (Rom 15:16).

Perhaps the greatest grant God could give to us is eternal life (Matt 19:29), the very thing we lost in the Garden of Eden. Of course, eternal life was granted in the OT, but the legal basis of this was not put into effect until Christ's death. This is why many graves of OT saints were opened (Matt 27:52-53), the moment Jesus died.

Inheritance

Many of these things we are said to "inherit." Again we can think of Hebrew's "will." But there are other ways of thinking about this too. Paul refers to eternal life especially in Romans 5:15, 17 (taking it from Jesus in John; cf. John 4:10) as "the gift." It is "the gift of God." The Apostle explains the gift this way. "But the free gift is not like the trespass. For if many died through one man's trespass, much more having the grace of God and the free gift by the grace of that one man Jesus Christ abounded for many" (Rom 5:15). He adds, "the free gift following many trespasses brought justification" (5:16), and "those who receive the abundance of grace and the free gift of righteousness reign in life through the one man Jesus Christ" (5:17), and "one act of righteousness leads to justification and life for all men" (5:18), and "by one man's obedience the many will be made righteous" (5:19), and grace reigns "through righteousness leading to eternal life through Jesus Christ our Lord" (5:21). Thus, the gift contains *justification* (being declared righteous), *righteousness* (Christ's righteousness imputed or credited to our account as well as a new, alien righteousness that we now live in via union with Christ), life (as in eternal life) and all of this comes by grace, rather than as the just penalty deserved because of sin.

The OT actually anticipates this covenant grant, this gracious gift of Jesus. A couple of passages in the LXX use the same word for gift as an adverb rather than a noun. One says, "For thus says the Lord, 'You have been sold for noth-ing [i.e. without cost]; and you shall not be ransomed with silver'" (Isa 52:3 LXX). "Nothing" (*dorea* in the LXX) is the same root word as "gift" (*dorean*) that Paul uses. How will God ransom them back? This passage introduces us to the greatest of all the Servant Songs in Isaiah, the great prediction of Jesus dying on the cross.[99]

New Creation: Covenant of Rest

Perhaps more clear is this passage: "If you buy a Hebrew servant, six years shall he serve you, and in the seventh year he shall go forth <u>free</u> for nothing" (Ex 21:2 LXX). "Free" (*dorea*) is the word "gift" (*dorean*). This is actually a very helpful transitional verse for returning to our idea of viewing covenants through the metaphor of a new creation "week," where each of the six old covenants represent a new unfolding of the work of God in redemption. These six old covenants climax in the final work of Jesus, in the eleventh hour of that sixth day, when he cried out to his Father, "It is finished" (John 19:30). What was finished? All of the work he had been sent to do.

What then was ushered in at that moment? The new covenant in his blood (Luke 22:20; 1 Cor 11:25; Heb 12:24). For this is the final and great sacrifice that atones for sin. Regarding the week idea, this new covenant is referred to as a covenant of "rest," just like the seventh day is in the old covenant. In fact, it is actually viewed as the *very same* rest, as opposed to a whole new rest (see below). To put it another way, the seventh day of Genesis 1 had no ending. It is unlike the

---

[99] Isa 52:13-53:12.

other six days.[100] In this way the old covenants lead people typologically and via the forbearance of God into the very presence of Christ through faith. For there is no difference. Abraham was saved by faith in the same promises and Lord that we trust in today. Let's look more specifically at this idea of the new covenant and its relation to rest (or "sabbath" in the Hebrew).

Consider how both David and Moses made a house for God. David said, "Hear me, my brothers and my people. I had it in my heart to build a house of rest for the ark of the covenant of the LORD and for the footstool of our God, and I made preparations for building" (1 Chr 28:2). Similarly, Hebrews says that "Moses also was faithful in all God's house" (Heb 3:2) which he built.[101]

Also, Christ has built a better house and thus it applies a "how much more" argument to us who spurn the gift of God through Christ and refuse to enter his "rest!" "Today, if you hear his voice, do not harden your hearts as in the rebellion, on the day of testing in the wilderness, where your fathers put me to the test and saw my works for forty years. Therefore I was provoked with that generation, and said, 'They always go astray in their heart; they have not known my ways.' As I swore in my wrath, 'They shall not enter my rest'" (Heb 3:7-12). This "rest" goes all the way back to Genesis 2:2 when God "rested" from his work.

---

[100] Note how the "morning and evening" formulas present in the first six days does not exist on the seventh day. The Psalms and Hebrews both pick up on this saying that this is the same rest the people of God can always enter into by faith.

[101] Cf. The seven "just as the LORD had commanded Moses" phrases concerning the building of the tabernacle in Ex 39:1, 5, 7, 21, 26, 29, 31 culminating in the eighth final summary in vs. 32.

"Rest" thus becomes the overarching theme of the next two chapters, being repeated in eight more verses of Hebrews 3-4. In this way, the Scripture refers to the new covenant as the ultimate rest that a person enters into. For now we know that all of our works are judged by God in Christ and we are justified. Now we know that our obedience to the commands of God can be performed in freedom and without fear of retribution if we fail, if we continually keep our faith fixed on Christ, the author and finisher of our faith (Heb 12:2).

New Covenant Consummated

We have seen that the New Covenant is here today. And yet, there is a real sense in which it is *not* here today. This fact and the inability to grasp it properly has led to a host of practical misapplications. First, it needs to be understood that the new heavens and earth are wrapped up in the new covenant.

New Heavens and New Earth

In Hebrews 12:24, Jesus is the mediator of a new covenant. Therefore, we must not refuse him who is speaking. "For if they did not escape when they refused him who warned them on earth, much less will we escape if we reject him who warns from heaven." Then it says, "At that time his voice shook the earth, but now he has promised, 'Yet once more I will shake not only the earth but also the heavens'" (Heb 12:25-26). This prediction goes back to Haggai 2:6ff. In that passage we see the treasures of "all nations" filling the house of God, and the glory of God fills the house with a greater glory than ever before. This similar kind of prediction is made throughout the OT prophets, and thus we see the connection between the new covenant and the new heavens and new earth, the church as Christ's temple, and those who dwell therein.

If this is true, and the new heavens and new earth are not here yet, then there must be some sense in which the new covenant is not yet fully realized. Theologians refer to this as the *already-not yet* and we have seen it before in this study. This *already-not yet* places us in a strange tension, not unlike the tension of Israel when they were no longer in Egypt, but not yet in Canaan. They were in the wilderness.

Our situation is different, of course. In one sense we are in the land flowing with milk and honey, as we have been raised and seated with Christ (Eph 2:6). Spiritually, via our mystical union with Jesus Christ (our head), we are in heaven! Given this tension, and given the same kind of tension between the basic continuity between the testaments yet clear discontinuity in key places, how are we to think practically about covenant theology? Let's turn our attention now to this final part of our study.

Applications of Covenant Theology

(*Why Does It Matter?*)

"THIS IS ALL VERY GOOD HEAD KNOWLEDGE," someone might say, "but who cares?" I hope that you are not saying that, but that instead you have been swept up in the great plan of God for your redemption. Still, we do want to begin answering this question. Understanding the story of the Bible by using the Bible itself to unfold it to us through one of its chief categories (i.e. covenants) ought to have an overwhelming effect on our life. It ought to make us stand in awe and revere a God who would go to such lengths as to save us from ourselves while we continued in our rebellion.

Worship

Thus, worship is perhaps the chief of all applications for thinking about a study like this. Covenant theology should drive us to praise. When we are led to worship we are fulfilling our "chief end." As the Larger Catechism puts it, "*The chief end of man is to glorify God and enjoy him forever.*" Worship is our first duty or obedience to God, but it only rightly flows from a changed heart, one that God has made anew, one that has repented of its sins and continues to do so throughout its existence on this earth. I hope that such a study has helped you worship God better.

But how are we to worship? With a basic unity of Scripture as a starting point, covenant theologians asked this question long ago. Let's consider worship as a moral duty. Isn't this what the 10 Commandments teach? "You shall have no other gods before me" (Ex 20:3; Deut 5:7). "You shall not make for yourself a carved image, or any likeness of anything that is in heaven above, or that is in the earth beneath, or that is in the water under the earth. You shall not bow down to them or serve them ..." (Ex 20:4-6; Deut 5:8-10). "You shall not take the name of the LORD your God in vain, for the LORD will not hold him guiltless who takes his name in vain" (Ex 20:7; Deut 5:11). "Observe the Sabbath day, to keep it holy, as the LORD your God commanded you" (Ex 20:8; Deut 5:12). Each of these duties continue to apply today.

These first four commandments show our obligation to God, obligation that should come from faith working itself out in love. We are to love the Lord our God with all our heart, soul, mind, and strength (Mark 12:30). This is worship. These first four commands deal with both private and public worship. As we have just spoken of private worship, we will look at the public aspect here.

To many outside of the Reformed tradition, two of the most controversial Reformed practices of worship flow out of applied covenant theology. These are the so called "Regulative Principle" of worship and the adherence to some form of keeping a weekly day of rest (Sabbath) on the "Lord's Day" (the first day of the week) set apart for the public worship of God. In both of these there is continuity and discontinuity with the OT.

The continuity is that the same basic principles apply today because they are moral law, and moral law remains in place forever. It is never right to take a life unlawfully as the sixth commandment teaches. It is never right to covet. And it is never right to worship God unacceptably, in a way that does not please him. The discontinuity does not come from the principle, but the application made in the NT temple.

Regulated Worship

The Regulative Principle is the idea that God decides the means, or technically the "elements" by which he is to be worshipped. God wants us to do what he has commanded us to do, especially in corporate worship.

An element is an appointed means whereby God has promised in his word that the grace of faith is crafted and shaped in the heart of a Christian. These include 1) the reading of the Scriptures, 2) preaching and hearing the Word of God, 3) singing psalms, hymns, and spiritual songs to the Lord, 4) prayer with thanksgiving for all things lawful, and 5) the administration of the sacraments (*1689 London Baptist Confession* 22.5).

These differ from "circumstances" which are things "common to human actions and societies, which are to be ordered by the light of nature and Christian prudence, according to the general rules of the Word" (*1689 London Baptist Confession* 1.6). As someone has put it, "The circumstances of worship would include place, time of day, length of the service, pews verses chairs, printed order or not, hymnals verses sheets or overhead transparencies, air conditioning verses fans, types of musical instruments, etc."[102]

---

[102] "A Position Paper Concerning the Regulative Principle of Worship: A Report by the Theology Committee of the Association of Reformed Baptist Churches of America (Formally Approved by the General Assembly March 8, 2001),

The elements of worship need a positive command from God, since they are the only things he has actually promised to use to create and strengthen faith in the heart. We should consider that worship is for him after all, and since only he knows how he should be worshiped, it is a reasonable principle to hold, especially given how angry he got throughout the OT when people did the wrong thing in worship, things not commanded, and sometimes not even forbidden (and let's not forget the NT warnings as well, such things as Ananias and Sapphira [Acts 5:1ff] and the Corinthian Christians falling dead [1 Cor 11:27-30] because of inappropriate acts of worship).

The principle comes from the Second Commandment (see above) and can be summarized this way, "You shall not worship the LORD your God in that way, for every abominable thing that the LORD hates they have done for their gods, for they even burn their sons and their daughters in the fire to their gods. Everything that I command you, you shall be careful to do. You shall not add to it or take from it" (Deut 12:31-32).

Israel's worship included all five of the elements listed above, but it also included other things such as animal sacrifices. There is, of course, discontinuity here. We do not worship with animal sacrifices anymore. But we do worship through the one sacrifice of Jesus Christ (Heb 9:26). We do not worship at a temple in Jerusalem (John 4:21). Yet, we go boldly into the heavenly throne of grace (Heb 4:16). This is still temple worship and we still offer sacrifices, but they are

http://s3.amazonaws.com/churchplantmedia-cms/arbca_carlisle_pa/regulative-principle.pdf, last accessed 10-14-2014.

sacrifices of a different kind. Our prayers are incense to God (Rev 5:8), our lives are "living sacrifices" (Rom 12:1-2), our proclamation of the Gospel is a priestly duty (Rom 15:16), and so on. Thus, it is critical from a covenant perspective to know how God was worshiped in the OT if we want to begin to see the continuity and discontinuity between the two ages.

This principle is quite different from a principle that is built more on discontinuity. The common way of worshiping God today is through what has been called the Normative Principle. It teaches that unless God has forbidden it, we are allowed to do it. We are not talking about circumstances here, but elements. Thus, all kinds of elements have been introduced into corporate worship in the name of this principle, as people add elements that they think will help God dispense grace. One thinks of how vital it is in some churches to play sentimental music while people walk down an aisle and pray to receive Christ at an anxious bench, or how in other traditions, it is has become imperative to have candles, rosaries, pictures, statues, and other objects in order to worship God best. These things are intended to bring grace and strengthen faith, though they have not been commanded by him, and are sometimes even forbidden.

The implications can be vast, but on the whole, we find that churches regulated by positive commands are much more simple in style, refuse to eliminate commanded elements, and teach the people to trust in God's means whereby he has promised to save them. This helps them be less prone to the tidal shifts of an ever ebbing culture where "change" is the only thing that seems to be good. It helps people anchor in that which is unchanging, to rely and trust not on human means and techniques, but upon the promises of God. This, of course, also remembers that outward expressions alone are not enough, for God cares about the heart just as much. It is by faith that we worship God in the way he desires. This is the heart of the Covenant of Grace.

Sabbath

The Sabbath idea is similar. Sabbath ("rest") is a moral duty, imbedded in the very fabric of creation. God rests on the seventh day (Gen 2:2-3), in part, as an example for us. This is reconfirmed to Israel in the fourth commandment. Yet, the idea of resting during a period of "seven" is found long before the Mosaic law. The story of Noah (whose name means "rest") is full of this kind of Sabbath significance (Gen 7:2, 3, 4, 10, 11; 8:4, 10, 12). The story of Jacob and Laban has it (Gen 29:20, 27, 30; cf. 50:3, 10). The story of Joseph has it (Gen 41:4-54). We even find it in pagan stories, such as the Baal cycle where his house is completed in seven days and the god is enthroned above his creation. This parallels Genesis almost exactly.[103]

Because of the continuity and the unending quality of God's original day of rest, we still enter God's rest ... today. The already/not yet means that we cannot say that God's rest is merely a "spiritual" reality, and that literal Sabbath wor-

---

[103] See Baal's House (KTU 1.4 vi 17-38; cf. Gudea Cylinders 617-624; Memphite Theology Col. 61) and my sermons Temple Building: Genesis 1:3-2:3 (http://www.rbcnc.com/Genesis%201.3-2.4%20Temple%20Building.pdf, last accessed 10-14-2014) and Sabbath Enthronement: Genesis 2:1-3 (http://www.rbcnc.com/Genesis%202.1-3%20Sabbath%20Enthronement.pdf, last accessed 10-14-2014).

ship is passé. Christianity is not Gnosticism which discards the physical for the spiritual.

We are still commanded not to forsake gathering together in church (Heb 10:25). "Church" actually means "assembly." We follow the example of the first Christians who did so on the Lord's Day (Acts 20:7; 1 Cor 16:2; Rev 1:10), which in the early church meant the first day of the week,[104] the day of Christ's resurrection.

This is in step with the typology and prophecy from the OT. Isaiah says that even in heaven we will continue to gather "from Sabbath to Sabbath" to worship the Lord (Isa 66:23). Why should that be suspended today? The typology of the first day (Ex 12:16; Num 1:18; Neh 8:2); eighth day (Gen 17:12 and circumcision; Lev 23:36; Num 29:35; 2 Chr 7:9; Neh 8:18); fifteenth day (Lev 23:6-7; 39); and fiftieth (Lev 25:6ff.)—with eight, fifteen, and fifty each starting a new cycle of "sevens"—were seen as being fulfilled in the church's gathering to celebrate the resurrection,[105] which is the beginning of the new creation when the true circumcision of the eighth day begins.[106] The church understood the Christian Sabbath to be a feast day fulfilling the first/eighth day feast-sabbaths of the OT.

---

[104] See *Paschal Canon* 11; *Decrees of Fabian: Decrees of the Same* 1; The *Prosphonesus of Theophilus* Canon 1; *Canons of the Synod of Laodacia* 29; *Teaching of the Twelve Apostles* 14; etc. in the Early Church Fathers.

[105] For first day resurrection see Matt 28:1ff; Mark 16:9; Luke 24:1ff; John 20:1ff. In the early church cf. Ignatius, *Magnesians* 9.

[106] For eighth day and the new creation: "What is the octave? It is the day of the Lord's resurrection on which we receive the fruit of our labors" Athanasius [*Treatise on the Psalms*]; cf. Eusebius of Caesarea [*Commentary on the Psalms*]; CCC Part 1, Sec. 2, Ch. 1, Art. 1, Para 5.2.349. On circumcision, the eighth day and/or the Christian sabbath: Barn 15:8-9; Didymus the Blind, *Fragments on the Psalms* 6.1; Augustine, *on Psalm 12.*

It is important to remember here that *sabbath* does not mean "seven," but "rest" (however, the "seven" principle still applies as the 6 + 1 principle is turned into a 1 + 6). The NT teaches us which day that rest is to occur in honor of the eschatology reality—the "already"—that we find ourselves in now because of the resurrection. Exactly how much continuity exists with the OT rules and regulations is a question for another time. Here we simply want to point out the principle again. Covenant theology shows us that if we want to make proper application, we need to first regard the continuity of the whole Scripture. Then, and only then, should we go to the NT to see how it might change things in accordance with the new covenant and kingdom of Christ. It will not do to just say that the NT doesn't repeat it so it is obsolete (which isn't true anyway). This is true of both the principle in the OT as well as the faith that they also needed in order to please God in their obedience.

How We Understand the Bible

This leads to another practical consideration regarding the focus of our Scripture reading. Covenant theology is not merely a doctrinal proposition or theoretical idea from the ivory tower. It is *a way of reading Scripture*. At the heart of Scripture is God's relationship to man. As I have shown, this relationship comes through God covenanting with us. This relationship is God's self-disclosure to us through his word (his oath, his covenant, his precepts) and his Word. When we think "Word" we are to think first and foremost of Jesus Christ. To put that more succinctly, Jesus is the focus of

Scripture—all of it. Other systems see this too, but covenant theology adds its own unique perspective.

The Bible is not a book of moral lessons, dos and don'ts, or even abstract theological propositions. It is a book of God's relationship to his creation through Jesus Christ the Mediator. These covenants between God and men were not just given by the Father, but through the Son in the power of the Holy Spirit. "Through the Son" can be abstract, so let me make it a little more concrete by returning to an idea we introduced with the call of Samuel.

On the day that God made a covenant with Abram, he "appeared" to the man "in a vision" (Gen 15:1). Here God is called "the word/Word ..." The Word brought Abram "outside" (15:5), implying some kind of physicality, even if it was a vision. Then the Word walked between the pieces of the severed animals (15:17), thereby swearing an oath that should he fail to make even one of the promises come to pass, that this should be his end too.

During the covenant ceremony on Mt. Sinai, when Moses, Aaron and his sons, and the seventy elders of Israel went onto the mountain it says "and they saw the God of Israel ... they beheld God, and ate and drank" (Ex 29:10-11). Later, this same God whom they beheld—"The angel of the LORD" (Jdg 2:1) said to their descendants, "I brought you up from Egypt and brought you into the land that I swore to give to your fathers. I said, 'I will never break my covenant with you ... but you have not obeyed my voice ... As soon as the angel of the LORD spoke these words to all the people of Israel, the people lifted up their voices and wept'" (Jdg 2:1-4).

Who covenanted with Israel except God alone? Yet, here is an Angel saying that he is the one who covenanted with them? Who can see God? Yet, here we see the elders of Israel beholding God. Here we see Abram seeing God in a vision. We see God being physically active, even if it is a vision. All of this is because this person they are seeing is the preincarnate Lord, the Second Person of the Holy Trinity. He is the one who was given Israel to be his inheritance among all the nations of the earth (Deut 29:7-9). This was temporary as he would soon inherit the nations (Ps 2:8; 82:8).

Scripture is about Jesus, because Jesus is there throughout the Scripture. He is the covenant God of the entire OT. But in the NT, he appears *in the flesh* having come down from heaven in the womb of the virgin, thereby adding a new nature unto himself. Covenant theology allows us to see this much more clearly through the covenantal promise of the seed and through the various covenants of prophet, priest, and king. Because of it, it prevents us from making huge errors such as turning the God of the OT against Jesus in the NT; or seeing the covenant God of Israel as some different person as the covenant Jesus of the NT; or seeing radical discontinuity in the law which the same Jesus gave in both testaments; or seeing different ways of salvation throughout different epochs of history. I want to turn your attention to this last one as we move to the next application.

How God Saves Sinners

C. I. Scofield forever changed the way many Protestants understood salvation in the Old Testament. He wrote for instance, "The righteous man under law became righteous by doing righteously; under grace he does righteously because he has been made righteous."[107] He also wrote, "As a dispensation, grace begins with the death and resurrection of Christ … The point of testing is no longer legal obedience as the conditions of salvation, but acceptance or rejection of Christ, with good works as a fruit of salvation."[108] Scofield was a Dispensationalist, and as we have suggested, Dispensationalism has as its basic hermeneutical principle—discontinuity.

Early Dispensationalism was a radical discontinuity, so much so in some places that it taught that those in the OT were saved by works. Recent Dispensationalism has rejected this obvious error, but such an error would never have occurred if a few things were present at the beginning. 1. Jesus is in the OT. 2. Jesus is making covenants with Israel. 3. Jesus is giving the law to Israel. 4. Jesus always saves people the same way (something covenant theology helps us understand). This last lesson is made clearest in Romans 4, where, thankfully, Scofield seems to have inconsistently said that Abraham was actually saved by faith.

The point is, covenant theology is a strong safeguard against such thinking. While it was not necessary that Dispensationalists would teach a different way of salvation, it certainly did happen. But we never see anything like this in the history of covenant theology for obvious reasons. The continuity of Scripture, the sameness of God, the one people of God through election, the unified purposes of God, the

---

[107] Scofield Study Notes from 1917; 1 John 3:7.
 http://www.biblestudytools.com/commentaries/scofield-reference-notes/genesis/genesis-15.html, last accessed 10-14-2014.
[108] Scofield Study Notes; John 1:17. Same link.

way God comes to mankind ... all of this helps to prevent aberrations regarding how someone is saved, either in the OT or in the NT.

The two historical covenants—works and grace also help to clarify what is otherwise muddy. What Scofield, Dispensationalists in general, and even New Covenant theologians sometimes get mixed up on is the relationship of law to grace. Some throw OT law (see below). Some throw law out altogether. Others throw it out only to replace it with an exact replica. That is, we keep the sixth commandment "do not murder," not because it was given to Moses, but because Jesus replaced it with an exact replica.[109] Covenant theology has a category for keeping the two side by side without mixing them together or destroying one or the other. Law has its place, both yesterday and today. Grace does too. But the grace dispensed in the OT is now vindicated by the death of Jesus Christ. Covenant theology helps us see these important distinctions so that we will be less prone to mess up God's word or our obedience in accordance with it.

Replacement Theology?

While talking about Dispensationalism, I want to bring out a common objection that has practical political implications if not also eschatological implications. It has to do with the charge by Dispensationalists that covenant theology is "*replacement* theology." What does this mean? The claim is

---

[109] Some will say that Jesus actually intensified the law so that "do not murder" becomes "do not even hate." But Jesus is getting the idea of not hating your brother from the OT law (cf. Lev 19:17). He isn't making it up. He is showing that all along this was the heart of the commandment.

made that we are teaching that the church replaces Israel in God's plan of redemption. In its most extreme forms, this charge associates covenant theology with anti-Semitism. This is a harmful caricature.

There is nothing here that can even be implied that covenant theology hates Jews. Instead, we have argued that God loves all people, and that he saves whomever he wants. This salvation began with *Jewish* people, as Jesus and all of the Apostles were ... *Jews*. The problem is that those who make such a charge have failed to understand what national Israel was in the first place. As Paul says, it was the vehicle through which the promises of God to the world would come (Rom 9:1-5). It was a type. It was real and physical, but it pointed beyond itself.

Curiously, the idea of Israel has never been completely bound to racial lines. This was typified early on in the Exodus when a mighty host—a mixed multitude (Ex 12:38)— left Egypt. From almost the beginning, there was no such thing as a pure Jew, as there was mixing and merging with the nations around them even as early as Joseph's sons Ephraim and Manasseh, both of an Egyptian mother. Moses' children were half Midianite. Then we have Gentiles like Rahab and Ruth who not only become Israelites (even though they are not Jewish), but even end up in the lineage of Jesus.

The most important thing of all in this regard is Jesus himself. Jesus becomes True Israel in his obedience. This can be seen in the way Matthew describes the life of Jesus as being born under the threat of death by a mad king bent on killing all the newborn babies two years and younger, going down to Egypt, coming out through a baptism, going into the wilderness to be tempted for a period of "forty," and finally ascending to a mountain to give the law. Jesus is also the Vine, (John 15:1ff), an image which Isaiah uses to describe Israel (Isa 5:1-7). We could list other OT links between Jesus and Israel as well. It seems to me it is a failure of epic proportions to miss this, thereby causing us to remain in types and shadows when the light is right before our eyes.

What about national Israel today? Covenant theology continues to recognize that there is such a thing as ethnic Israel, just as it recognizes that Kenyans, Swedes, and Koreans are their own national groups. Some covenant theologians even believe God might very well do something to save a large number of ethnic Jews in the last days; there is nothing inherent in the system that would militate against this. What covenant theology refuses to do is go back to types and shadows, thereby replacing Christ who is The Temple and True Israel and True Sacrifice, with a national entity that will reestablish a sacrificial system in a man-made temple. Animals, physical temples, and nations have fulfilled their purposes in the plan of redemption, for they all find their end focus in Jesus who brings a new heavenly kingdom along with his spiritual temple and spiritual sacrifices that we offer in Christ.

No, this isn't replacement, but fulfillment. Thus, someone has written, "It is, therefore, not the case of one people replacing another people, but the case of one covenant replacing another covenant when the promise revealed by the Covenant of Grace from Genesis 3:15 on were accomplished, when the Old Covenant ended and a large group made up of Jews and non-Jews entered into the New Covenant. One must refuse the opposition between Israel and the Church and rather emphasize the scope of the Covenant of Grace in the Old Testament (Israel) and the scope of the Covenant of

Grace in the New Testament (every nation). The Gentiles do not replace Israel, but are added as inheritors of the blessings of Israel. The opposition that is found in the New Testament is between the Old and New Covenants and not between Israel and the Church, which is rather an artificial opposition coming from Dispensationalism."[110]

How to Understand the Law

I have looked at the Sabbath and at the idea of law in general. I want to get a little more specific here as we think about the law from the perspective of covenant theology (and, we believe, the Bible) and more application. One of the great hallmarks of Reformed Theology is its clear distinction between law and gospel. The law promises upon obedience and threatens upon disobedience. The law actually creates and increases sin in the heart (Rom 5:20; 7:7-11), even if its threatenings keep people from committing certain acts outwardly. Have you ever watched a child when you tell them that now they *must* take a nap?

To any lawbreaker (and that would be all of us), the law's threats can only terrify, bring fear, punishment, curse, and death ... unless, you see in that law your need for grace and salvation from outside of yourself. This is where grace comes in through the gospel. The law was (and remains) a tutor to bring people to Christ (Gal 3:24). But Christ is the end of the law for all who believe (Rom 10:4). It is not that the law goes away, but that its function to bring us to justifying

---

[110] Pascal Denault, *The Distinctiveness of the Baptist Covenant Theology* (Vestavia Hills, AL: Solid Ground Christian Books, 2013), 75.

faith in Christ goes away. Its threats of eternal damnation go away. But the righteousness of God displayed in the law never goes away. "The law is holy, righteous, and good" (Rom 7:12). And sin is law*less*ness (1 John 3:4). If there is no law in the NT, then there can't be any sin either. Sin makes no sense apart from law.

People know this inherently, but often times their theology denies it. How often I have heard Paul's, "We are not under law, but under grace" (Rom 6:14) taken to mean, "The law is useless to believers, of little value today, and can be largely discarded," even though the very next verse says "by no means" should we sin so that grace will increase (6:15), and they themselves usually abhor sin too. In another place he says, "We uphold the law" (Rom 3:31). Thus, in a sanctifying sense, the law continues to drive us to rely solely on Christ, even as it becomes for us a light that we desire to walk by.

Sometimes people will say that we are no longer under the Ten Commandments. Yet, they will say that we are under the Nine Commandments—all except the Sabbath (see above for the Sabbath discussion). Where would such an idea come from? It certainly doesn't come from a proof-text. It comes from a system. It comes from an absence. "The NT repeats nine but not ten of the Commandments," we are told. (This assumes, of course, that the NT does *not* actually repeat the Sabbath commandment.)[111]

---

[111] Jesus refers to the Sabbath regularly and never broke it, though the Pharisees accused him of breaking it. Paul relists the 10 commandments to Timothy in 1 Timothy 1:8-10 where "profane" equates to a Sabbath breaker. And the passages where Paul refers to certain OT holy days (Rom 14:6; Col 2:16; etc.) are not talking about the fifth commandment. I won't defend this here, but the point is, if you have continuity (via covenants) in

But it does more. It possibly assumes that Jesus did not give the Law to Moses in the OT. Have you ever heard of the "Red Letter Bible?" Note that there are no red letters in the OT in those Bibles. Jesus is clearly absent. It definitely assumes that the moral law has been abrogated, even though Jesus clearly says he did not come to do that, "I have not come to abolish the law" (Matt 5:17). Strangely, though Jesus says this, it is sometimes claimed that when he continues, "... but to fulfill it," that this in fact means he did come to abolish it.[112] Whatever "fulfill" means, Jesus is pointing out it does *not* mean abolish. But again, covenant theology does not lead to such strange conclusions, and this is why you never find any of its adherents arguing for such things. There is obviously a lot more I could say, but it should be clear that covenant theology helps us understand our relationship to the law quite differently (and I believe, much more biblically) than other systems.

How We Practice Baptism and the Lord's Supper

The next application returns us to the idea of worship, especially, corporate worship. It is the idea of the Lord's Supper and Baptism. These are two of the "elements" of worship

---

mind at the outset, then it doesn't even come into the mind that God would overthrow one of the Ten Commandments. Certainly, there is discontinuity here, but also continuity.

[112] As an example, the usually fine exegete D. A. Carson writes about this preface of Jesus to the Sermon on the Mount that, "Jesus' mission was not to abolish ... the law or the prophets," but then adds in one of its specific applications, "If oaths designed to encourage truthfulness become occasions for clever lies and casuistical deceit, Jesus will abolish oaths." D. A. Carson, "Matthew," in *The Expositor's Bible Commentary, Volume 8: Matthew, Mark, Luke*, ed. Frank E. Gaebelein (Grand Rapids, MI: Zondervan Publishing House, 1984), 142, 153.

we discussed above. The Reformed have traditionally referred to these as "sacraments," from the Latin word meaning "mystery." Though the Roman Catholic Church teaches that sacraments work *ex opere operato* (by the fact that it is performed), and on the basis of the faith of the church for the person receiving it, this is a corruption of the original idea.

The mystery of the sacraments has been defined by Augustine and others as an "invisible grace" that comes from the outward sign when it is received by personal faith of the one receiving it. Our Confession of Faith speaks of this as a "means of grace" (*London Baptist Confession* 18.3; cf. 14.1; 22.5), not as justifying or "saving grace," but rather as *sanctifying* grace. They help strengthen, nourish, and grow the faith that has already been established through the gospel. Why would they do this? It is because they are the gospel in *visible* form.

The Bible says that "the gospel is the power of God unto salvation…" (Rom 1:16; cf. Eph 1:13). What is the gospel? It is the declaration that Jesus Christ has died for our sin and been raised to life for our justification (Rom 4:25). And, "Whoever confesses with their mouth that Jesus is Lord and believes in their heart that God raised him from the dead will be saved" (Rom 10:9). It is not about what I have done (believed or received), but what Christ has done for me.

Baptism and the Lord's Supper proclaim this same message. They proclaim his body crucified (Luke 22:19-20; 1 Cor 11:24-26), dead, buried, and raised again (Rom 6:3-4). They are not about what I do, but what he has done. Therefore, they are the Gospel. But they are the Gospel to our senses (touch, taste, smell, hear, see), and belong to those who have first received faith.

God illustrated this for us in the tabernacle wherein lay, in the Most Holy Place, the Ark of the *Covenant*. It was the repository and house of God's covenant. The priest alone could go into the outer Holy Place of the tabernacle, and only the high priest could go into the Most Holy Place. Prior to entry, he had to be washed in water in his initiation ceremony and then clothed with his priestly robes (Ex 29:4-9). Once he met the qualifications, then he was washed or baptized.[113] Then, and only then, could he go into the Holy Place where, upon entry, he would see the bread and the wine laid out before him. Let's talk a bit more about these two things, for here we have our two sacraments of the sanctuary.

Baptism

Understanding covenant theology properly helps us understand baptism properly. Often times it is argued—from covenant theologians—that baptism is to be performed by *sprinkling* upon believers *and their children*. A proper understanding of covenant theology corrects this. The idea of sprinkling comes from certain ceremonial laws in the OT. These laws were baptisms,[114] but they do not correspond to the sacrament of Christian baptism.

Christian baptism comes from Jesus' baptism. As his was, so ours is. When Jesus was baptized, he was "fulfilling all righteousness" (Matt 3:15), which in Matthew's gospel al-

---

[113] See Douglas Van Dorn, *Waters of Creation* (Erie, CO: Waters of Creation Publishing, 2009).

[114] Heb 9:10 refers to the "diverse washings (*baptismos*)" of the Levitical covenant.

ways means obeying the law.[115] Jesus was baptized at a determined age, when he was 30 (Luke 3:23). It was performed
by a very specific man, John the Baptist, a Levitical priest
(Luke 1:5; 13), immediately prior to his priestly ministry
(Luke 3:25). Why? Because Jesus' baptism was his initiation
ceremony into his priestly ministry according to the law of
the priesthood in Exodus 29:4-9. True, he was not in the line
of Levi, but Melchizedek (Ps 110:4; Heb 6:20; 7:11). But this
is because his priesthood had to be greater than Levi's. This is
the theme for several chapters of Hebrews, and it serves to
justify why Jesus is fulfilling *Aaronic-priestly* duties, just as he
is in his baptism, even though he is not a Levite.

In this ceremony, the priest was washed. This is the same
word used for the bathing of Bathsheba (2 Sam 11:2) and the
baptism of Naaman (2 Kgs 5:10; the only time the Greek
word appears in the LXX). In other words, this was no sprinkling or pouring. It was a bath. Baptism is a perfectly good
word to express it, for this is a dipping into and out of the
water. Fulfilling the imagery of the priestly ceremony is our
Christian baptism. Thus Paul says, "For all of you who were
<u>baptized</u> into Christ have <u>clothed</u> yourselves with Christ"
(Gal 3:27 NAS). That is the ordination ceremony of the
priest in a nutshell.

Remember, that the priests were given their own special
covenant in the OT. This ceremony was their initiation into
that covenant. In other words, the initiation of the priest into
the waters of baptism is to the Priestly Covenant what circumcision for an 8 day old male Jew was to the Abrahamic

---

[115] On "fulfill" having this OT meaning see Matt 1:22; 2:5; 15, 17, 23. On righteousness
talking about obeying the law see 3:15; 5:20; 6:1; 21:32 and probably 5:10.

covenant. But the two are not the same covenant (even though they both typify the covenant of grace).

This is critical for a correct understanding of who is to be baptized. The idea of baptizing infants comes from the incorrect identification of baptism as "replacing" circumcision.[116] This comes from the incorrect identification of seeing the Abrahamic covenant as Covenant of Grace. It isn't.

True, Abraham would be—by virtue of God's foreknowledge and forbearance—saved by Christ's blood in the Covenant of Grace, but we are not in the Abrahamic covenant. It doesn't work both ways, because the two are not identical. Paedobaptists understand this implicitly, which is why they talk about baptism replacing circumcision. Yet, this idea would have no legs if it weren't for the prior assumption that the Abrahamic covenant *is* the Covenant of Grace. As the old Reformed Baptist Hercules Collins wrote, "Those that argue for their infant-seeds baptism from circumcision being entailed unto Abraham's seed, may as well argue and say, the priesthood was by a covenant entailed on the tribe of Levi and his seed, therefore the ministry is entailed upon gospel-preachers and their seed: as this cannot be warranted, no more can the other."[117]

---

[116] Some Paedobaptists do not like this "replacement" language, yet this is the language of their own confessions and writers. The Belgic Confession, Article 34 says, "Having abolished circumcision, which was done with blood, [Jesus Christ] *established in its place* the sacrament of baptism." Thus, someone like Kim Riddlebarger says, "Baptism replaces circumcision." (Kim Riddlebarger, *The Sacraments: Lecture 4* – "Baptist Objections to Infant Baptism and the Reformed Response," at http://christreformedinfo.org/lecture-4/, last accessed 10-14-2014).

[117] Hercules Collins, *Believers-Baptism from Heaven* (London: J. Hancock, 1691) [spelling modernized].

Baptism and circumcision do have some things in common. But no one would confuse them as being the same ritual. Jesus was circumcised into the Abrahamic covenant (Luke 2:21), then he was baptized into the Priestly Covenant (and at the end of his life he would be coronated in a mocking way into the Davidic covenant). When we see distinct covenants, as the Bible does, it is plain as day that baptism does not replace circumcision, because baptism fulfills *baptism*. The reason why we do not baptize infants, then, has nothing to do with how we view our children (see Covenant Membership below). It has to do with the fact that infants cannot serve God as priests. But Christians can and do, as we have seen in this study. This is why we are a "priesthood of believers" (1 Pet 2:5, 9; Rev 5:10), or as Isaiah put it, Levitical priests (Isa 66:19-21), even though most of us are not even Jewish. This fact provides exegetical and covenantal reasons for why we never see infants baptized in the NT.

The Lord's Supper

So what about the Lord's Supper? How does covenant theology help us here? First, if we have the right view of baptism, then an increasingly popular view of the Supper will be off the table immediately. This is the so-called "paedocommunion." Like paedobaptism (the baptism of infants), this view seeks to give communion to any little child that has received baptism and is old enough to eat solid food. But this defeats the point of the priesthood and serving/guarding the sanctuary of God. NT priests are believers, those who profess faith in Christ. Yes, our faith ought to be like the faith of a child, but it is the *faith*, not the *child* that is the analogy. Can young children have a truly credible profession of faith? Yes, and as such, we might consider them for the Supper. But infants? No.

Covenant theology also enhances our view of the Supper more generally. As we have seen, covenants were often sealed with covenant meals. These meals were often bread and wine (Gen 14:18; Ex 24 (implied by the bread context); Isa 55:1-3; etc., which represent the animal sacrificed. If the Supper is for God's church where they partake in the Holy Place, then it is reasonable to assume that a major component of corporate worship is that it is a weekly reenactment of a covenant renewal ceremony. How much more if our Lord's Day worship is in fulfillment of the first/eighth day feast *sabbaths* of the OT!

Covenant renewal is common in the Scriptures. We have seen that the covenant with Abraham was renewed with Isaac, and again with Jacob. The covenant with Aaron was renewed with Phinehas. Even among individuals, God would often come to them in covenant more than one time. This happened with Noah, Abraham, Jacob, Moses, Israel, and more. The idea of a covenant renewal ceremony is found in places like Joshua 24. Here, the entire covenant is reenacted. It is read, its terms are agreed upon again, and so forth. Having the Supper weekly is a way to help people understand the broader context of worship, that God is coming again to renew his grace with those who confess their sins and trust in Christ by faith alone. Surely, we are not far away from this thought in Jesus' own words, "This cup that is poured out for you is the new covenant in my blood" (Luke 22:20), "Do this, as often as you drink it, in remembrance of me" (1 Cor 11:25).

Covenant Membership

We will conclude by looking at the controversial question of covenant membership. Who is "in" the new covenant? This is often one of the first places Paedobaptists turn in defending their views. As just pointed out, however, I believe it is irrelevant to the question of who receives baptism. If we don't presuppose circumcision as a connection, this becomes a moot point. Nevertheless, it is an important issue on its own merit.

Believers and the Elect

The first point we'll make is a semantic one. The NT speaks of the new covenant as being made with "believers." In trying to answer the question at hand, it is important to properly define the term "believer" and not to equivocate its meaning by defining it at one point as "all who profess Christ" and at another time as "the elect."

It is tempting to say that all of the elect are in the new covenant. However, we must remember that not all of the elect as of this moment believe. Some have not yet been brought to saving faith and some have not yet even been born. If we want to speak biblically, no one is in the new covenant until they profess faith, even if they are elect. They "will be" in the covenant at some point in time (because of the certainly of election), but not all are present in the covenant at this moment.

Furthermore, the term "believer" is sometimes used for falsely professing believers who are not elect, "believers" such as Simon the Sorcerer (Acts 8:13). Simon was baptized, because he "believed" (*pisteuo*). These kinds of believers are not united to Christ and the new covenant in a life-giving and vital way, but they do seem to be spoken of in an external, temporary way. This is not completely dissimilar to unbelieving Israel in the OT.

"Children" and "Infants" of the New Covenant

Next comes the idea of an infant's relationship to this covenant. Part of the Paedobaptist idea of baptizing infants is that baptism ushers the infant into membership in the covenant of grace. Some (Roman Catholics) say this membership saves the child. Others (Lutherans, Presbyterians) say it does not, though they can sometimes speak as if it does. It is often their taunt to Baptists, "Why do you hate your little children," by which they mean why do you keep them away from the means of grace through covenant membership by not baptizing them as infants?

Most Baptists will respond by admitting that our infants are not "in" the covenant of grace, for this covenant is made with believers only, and its eternal blessings will be given to the elect who were given to the Son by the Father before the foundation of the world. Yet, we do believe that our infants come "near" the covenant each time God's people gather together in the same way that falsely professing Christians and others who attend worship without ever confessing a thing come near. In fact, it is so near that they can "taste" of heavenly things (Hebrews 6), even if they cannot be filled with them. While we do not give them baptism and the Supper until they profess faith (because we do not want to heap added wrath upon them if they spurn it later on), we do acknowledge that hearing the word and seeing the means of grace, including fellowship and prayer, is a special, sacred thing, a thing that can result in external and temporary blessings, but a thing to which all of us will be held accountable if we then trample the Son of God underfoot.

Therefore, while most of us would not say that our infants are in the covenant, we certainly don't treat them like blasphemers and hypocrites either (and exactly how are we to treat these anyway?). We love our children. We treat them with kindness, in patience, with much longsuffering, with gentleness, and respect. We teach them of the absolute necessity of coming to faith in Christ. We pray for them. We raise them with the moral law of God. We allow them to come near to the means of grace by bringing them into our worship services. And we realize that they have been given a special common (though not saving) grace that God very often uses to bring them to Christ. There is nothing hateful about that.

One final point can be added to our answer. The NT does in fact teach that there are "children" in the covenant. It is just that it reserves the right to define who those children are, as all covenants do. In other covenants, the children are the children of the covenant head. The children in the Abrahamic covenant are sons of Abraham; the children in the Levitical covenant are sons of Aaron; the children in the Davidic covenant are sons of David; and so on.

In the new covenant, the children of the covenant are <u>sons</u> *of Christ* and to be his son you have to be "<u>born</u> again" (John 3:3-7). Jesus says, "Take heart, my <u>son</u>; your sins are forgiven" (Matt 9:2). He asked his disciples, "<u>Children</u>, do you have any fish?" (John 21:5). He says, "Little <u>children</u>, yet a little while I am with you" (John 13:33). The Apostle says,

"In Christ Jesus you are all <u>sons</u> of God, through faith" (Gal 3:26). Both Paul and John call the recipients of their letters "my little <u>children</u>" (Gal 4:19; 1 John 3:18). Peter warns his audience to be "obedient <u>children</u>" (1 Pet 1:14). The author of Hebrews says, "I will put my trust in him. And again, Behold I and the <u>children</u> God has given me" (Heb 2:13).

In fact, the NT even uses the language of "infants," not of biological infants, but of spiritual infants in Christ (1 Pet 2:2; cf. 1 Cor 3:2, 9:7; Heb 5:12-13). Who are these children, these infants? They are believers in Christ. Thus Jesus says, "Truly, I say to you, unless you turn and become like children, you will never enter the kingdom of heaven" (Matt 18:2). Indeed, the KJV calls us "<u>babes</u> *in Christ*" (1 Cor 3:1).

This is all typified in the OT, but it is only typological. Biological birth is typological of the new birth; it does not transfer to the new covenant. The NT makes clear, "If you were Abraham's children, you would be doing the works Abraham did" (John 8:39). How can this be? Because, "It is those of faith who are the sons of Abraham" (Gal 3:7). Through faith, he is the father of us all (Rom 4:16). To return to the idea of infants just being born automatically into the new covenant is to stay in the shadows of the old covenant. That doesn't mean these people can't come near the covenant and means of grace though. Indeed, they should.

Be Born Again

The greater point is that those who come into this covenant must be born again (John 3:3, 7; 1 Pet 1:3, 23). Have you been born again? Have you trusted in the promises made "Yes" and "Amen" in Christ? Have you become as a little

child, humbling yourself before the Heavenly Father? Have
you entered into the kingdom of God through faith in the
only begotten Son, who obeyed the Covenant of Works so
that he might offer you salvation and extend to you the eternal blessings of the Covenant of Grace? Repent of your sins
and trust in him alone; for there is no other name in heaven
or earth by which you can be saved. Do not let this be a mere
exercise of the mind. Engage your heart and affections too,
and let your whole body follow in covenantal obedience of
the God who saves anyone who comes to him by grace alone.

For those who have been born again, consider how covenant theology is able to deepen a real trust and rest in the
sovereignty of God. God doesn't have to rely on Plan B. He
knows it all, the end from the beginning. Incredibly, he has
chosen to let the story be played out through human beings.
God uses us, even though he doesn't need to and even when
we were in rebellion against him. What a surpassing comfort
such a through can bring. There are no surprises to God. He
is faithful in the great things and in the little things. He has a
purpose and we can rest in that purpose, because it involves
his gracious covenantal relationship which he will never go
against, thanks to Jesus Christ.

I hope that through this study you have been made
aware of the riches of the whole of God's word in new ways.
I trust you can see the practical applications of our theology
in everyday life. And I pray that God might use this study to
bring you to a closer walk with himself, through Jesus Christ
our Covenant Keeper and Maker, and through the glorious
Holy Spirit who breathes life into that covenant.

Select Works Cited

Augustine. "*A Treatise on the Spirit and the Letter* 53: Volition and Ability." In *A Select Library of the Nicene and Post-Nicene Fathers of the Christian Church, First Series, Volume V: Saint Augustin: Anti-Pelagian Writings*. Ed. Philip Schaff. Trans. Peter Holmes. New York: Christian Literature Company, 1887.

Blackburn, Earl M. "Covenant Theology Simplified." In *Covenant Theology: A Baptist Distinctive*, ed. Earl M. Blackburn. Birmingham, AL: Solid Ground Christian Books, 2013.

Boston, Thomas, *The Whole Works of the Late Reverend and Learned Mr. Thomas Boston*, 12 vols. Aberdeen: George and Robert King, 1848.

Bunyan, John. *Doctrine of the Law and Grace Unfolded*, vol. Bellingham, WA: Logos Bible Software, 2006.

Collins, Hercules. *Believers-Baptism from Heaven*. London: J. Hancock, 1691.

Conner Kevin J. and Malmin, Ken. *The Covenants: The Key to God's Relationship with Mankind*. Portland, OR: City Bible Publishing, 1997.

Coxe, Nehemiah. "A Discourse of the Covenants." In *Covenant Theology from Adam to Christ*. Palmdale, CA: Reformed Baptist Academic Press, 2005.

Dabney, Robert Lewis. *The Five Points of Calvinism*. Harrisonburg, VA: Sprinkle Pub, 1992.

_____. *Syllabus and Notes of the Course of Systematic and Polemic Theology*, second edition. St. Louis: Presbyterian Publishing Company, 1878.

Denault, Pascal. *The Distinctiveness of the Baptist Covenant Theology*. Vestavia Hills, AL: Solid Ground Christian Books, 2013.

Gonzales, Bob. "The Covenantal Context of the Fall: Did God Make a Primeval Covenant with Adam?" *Reformed Baptist Theological Review* 4.2 (July 2007): 4-32.

Malone, Fred. *The Baptism of Disciples Alone: A Covenantal Argument for Credobaptism Versus Paedobaptism*. Cape Coral, Fl.: Founders Press, 2003.

Manton, Thomas. "Sermons Upon 1 Peter 1:23." In *The Complete Works of Thomas Manton, vol. 21*. London: James Nisbet & Co., 1873.

Renihan, Micah and Renihan, Samuel. "Reformed Baptist Covenant Theology and Biblical Theology." In Richard C. Barcellos, ed. *Recovering a Covenantal Heritage: Essays in Baptist Covenant Theology*. Palmdale, CA: RBAP, 2014).

Shedd, William Greenough Thayer. *Dogmatic Theology*. Ed. Alan W. Gomes, 3rd ed. Phillipsburg, NJ: P & R Pub., 2003.

Smith, Henry B. *System of Christian Theology*, 2nd ed. New York: A.C. Armstrong and Son, 1884.

Trench, Richard Chenevix. *Synonyms of the New Testament*, 9th ed., improved. Bellingham, WA: Logos Bible Software, 2003: 219-25.

Van Dorn, Douglas. *Waters of Creation*. Erie, CO: Waters of Creation Publishing, 2009.

Watson, Thomas. *The Doctrine of Repentance*. Carlisle, PA: Banner of Truth Trust, 1987.

Scripture Index

Made in the USA
Coppell, TX
17 April 2023

15736709R00105